Architectural Design Procedures

Architectural Design Procedures

Arthur Thompson

MBIAT, Associate Member CIOB, Cert. Ed
Formerly Senior Lecturer, Vauxhall College

Edward Arnold
A division of Hodder & Stoughton
LONDON MELBOURNE AUCKLAND

© 1990 Arthur Thompson

First published in Great Britain 1990
Reprinted 1992

British Library Cataloguing in Publication Data

Thompson, Arthur
  Architectural design procedures.
  1. Architectural design – Manuals
  I. Title
  721

  ISBN 0–340–50413–7

Typeset in 10/11½pt Oracle by Colset Private Limited,
Singapore Printed and Bound in Great Britain for Edward
Arnold, a division of Hodder and Stoughton Limited, Mill
Road, Dunton Green, Sevenoaks TN13 2YA by J. W. Arrowsmith
Ltd., Bristol

Dedication

To my wife Jean

Preface

The practice of architecture and building design in this book is described in simple terms, explaining the way architects do their work, and how they integrate with the work of staff on construction sites. The various stages of the architect's job is explained, in line with the RIBA Plan of Work, from the time the architect is appointed by the client to the handing over of the finished building. The organisation and business side of architectural practices are covered, as are the constraints placed on the architect's design by factors such as legal implications. Examples of typical letters and standard forms are included, which would be useful for the case studies students are generally expected to undertake as part of their courses.

The text assumes no previous knowledge of the subject. It meets the requirements of Design Procedures NIII of the BTEC National Certificate in Building Studies, the Diploma in Construction, and the Diploma in Construction and Land Use. It would be a useful tool for student architects during the first part of their degree course, and architectural technician students on BTEC First Awards Certificate and Diploma courses. The book also provides an introduction to the British architectural profession for overseas students, including members of the EEC who expect to practise architecture in Britain.

The book has been arranged in the sequence which the author has found to be the most suitable when teaching the subject. There is a limited amount of deliberate repetition between some of the chapters to reinforce the student's learning of key items.

NB In outlining the roles of members of the building team, and elsewhere in this book, the word 'he' is used in a generic sense. All roles listed can be performed equally well by women and men. In fact, there is a gradual, but welcome trend for women to take on jobs in the construction industry.

Acknowledgements

The author is grateful to the Royal Institute of British Architects for permission to reproduce some of their standard forms, together with extracts from the Architect's Jobbook, and the CI/SfB Construction Indexing Manual. Copies of these publications are available from the RIBA Publications Limited.

Thanks are also offered to the British Institute of Architectural Technicians for permission to publish an extract from their 1988 Yearbook, and to the Royal Institution of Chartered Surveyors for information they supplied about their Building Cost Information Service, and to Barbour Index for information they supplied about their Microfile System.

Finally the author wishes to thank his wife for the help she gave to him over the period of preparation of this book, and in particular for checking the typescript.

Contents

List of figures and tables

1

Setting the scene

1.1 The beginning

Every building begins in the mind of one person. It may be someone wanting a home built for their family, or a speculator wishing to build a block of flats to sell for a profit. It may be a trader seeking a shop to dispose of their goods, or an industrialist needing a factory in which to manufacture products. It may be a Christian with ambition to create a building to advance their religious belief, or an enthusiastic golfer anxious to construct a golf clubhouse. The building may be required for pleasure, income, utilitarian uses, or many other purposes, but almost invariably the initial impetus comes from one person recognising a need and deciding to do something about it.

In most cases other people – family, friends, colleagues, associates – will soon become involved, and may even take over the idea of providing a particular building as being their own, and either jointly or by themselves assuming responsibility for commissioning the work.

At some stage too, the innovator, unless he possesses the necessary expertise in design and building – or thinks he does – will seek professional advice to help translate ideas into a completed building.

1.2 Enters the architect

Traditionally, the first person the innovator will generally turn to, although he may not always be quite sure what to expect, is the architect. Nowadays the practice of architecture is extremely complicated. Some see it as a combination of understanding different architectural styles, possessing artistic sense, and being able to create buildings which delight the eye. Others see it as possessing skills in construction technology and applying them to the design of buildings. In truth it is both these things, but to be really successful and efficient, architects, as well as having artistic and technological skills, also need at least a working knowledge of laws, regulations, customs, costs, business and much more.

Essentially however, the architect is employed by the client to act as his agent and see that he is provided with a building which will satisfy his needs. To achieve this, the architect, with the approval of the client, has to make a series of choices.

Firstly, she will be concerned that the building will satisfy the functional requirements of the occupants.

Secondly, she has to decide how to make the building attractive to look at. She will be concerned with massing, proportion, unity of the various parts, and choice of the right materials.

Thirdly, she will have to choose a suitable structural form, and appropriate finishes and services, taking care that the completed building will not incorporate any defects.

There will also be choices to be made which relate to costs. Often the architect's decisions will affect running costs and maintenance costs for the future life of the building. The architect will be concerned with many other practical matters, such as how to minimize the dangers and inconvenience of fire damage, noise transmission and thermal loss.

In all that the architect does, a decision will have to be made as to how the requirements of a complicated network of regulations, standards and legal require- ments are best met. Finally, the architect must choose how best to manage the actual building operations.

1.3 The building team

As well as possessing the multitude of talents outlined above, the architect should also possess the ability to work as a member of a team. Traditionally the architect is recognised as being the head of the building team, but relies on the assistance of others to translate design into a finished building.

The four main groups involved in the design and construction of a building are the client, the design team, the contracting team, and the statutory authorities. The roles of the key members are summarised below.

The client

The client is also known as the building owner, and in the building contract is generally referred to as the 'employer'. The client may be a single individual, a small private company, a large public limited company, a local authority, a state corporation, a voluntary society, and practically any other organisation you can think of.

Essentially the role of the client is to tell the architect of his requirements, commission the works, and either directly or indirectly 'employ' everyone on the project.

The design team

The architect
As has been mentioned, the role of the architect is to act as the client's agent in the design and supervision of the building, advising and guiding him as necessary, from inception of the initial idea to final completion and occupation of the finished building. His work will include the preparation of the design and drawings, and obtaining statutory approvals.

The architectural technician

The technician will assist the architect, particularly in respect of preparing the detailed drawings, but is often involved in all aspects of the work, including contract procedures and supervision. The division of responsibility will vary from office to office, but often the arrangement is for the architect to have responsibility for the overall design, and the technician to prepare the detailed drawings, schedules and specifications. This matter is dealt with in more detail in chapters 2 and 3.

The clerk of works

He is generally employed directly by the client, but acts as the architect's representative on site. Responsibilities of the clerk of works are limited to that of an inspector, without the power to issue instructions on his own authority.

The quantity surveyor

The quantity surveyor is employed by the client as his own, and the architect's advisor on anything relating to the cost of the job. Specific duties include preparing the bills of quantities, checking tenders, and carrying out valuations of costs during the progress of the job.

The consulting structural engineer

He is also employed by the client, as a member of the architect's team to assist in the design, construction and supervision of the structural elements in the building.

The resident engineer

He acts as the structural engineer's representative on the site.

The consulting building services engineer

He occupies a similar role to the structural engineer, but in respect of the building engineering services – i.e. lighting, heating, drainage etc.

The contracting team

The contractor or builder

He is employed by the client, on the advice of the architect, to construct the building in accordance with the drawings prepared by the design team.

The site manager

He is sometimes called the site agent, and is employed by the contractor to control the work on the site.

The contracts manager
He is employed by the contractor, generally to run a number of contracts. The contracts manager is the site manager's immediate supervisor, and may on a large contract, be permanently resident on site and given the title of project manager.

The site engineer
He is responsible for setting out and controlling the accuracy of the building work.

The sub-contractor
He is responsible, under the control of the contractor, for part of the construction work.

The supplier
He has responsibility for supplying materials used by the contractor in the building.

The Statutory Authorities

The building control officer
This person has responsibility for ensuring that the building is constructed in accordance with the building regulations, which should mean that, when the building is completed it will not be a danger to the health and safety of the occupants. This role may also be undertaken by an approved inspector, who is either a private individual, or employed by the National House Building Council.

The town planning officer
He is responsible for ensuring that the building is appropriate for the area in which it is built, and is of acceptable appearance.

1.4 Summary of main roles

It can be seen that most people involved in the building process can assume one of three main roles. These are:

(a) To provide the demand and the money – i.e. the client or employer.

(b) To design the building or help in this process – e.g. the architect and quantity surveyor.

(c) To help build – e.g. the contractor.

   The roles may be combined – for example, the contractor may also be the designer, the employer and contractor may combine, or all three roles may be undertaken by one organisation.

1.5 Main approaches to building

There are two main approaches to building. The first is speculative building in which an entrepreneur buys land and builds upon it, hoping to sell the finished building for profit. The best known example of this is the firm that builds and sells houses to the general public. Speculative building results in a contract of sale. The contract may, in the case of a house, be based on viewing the actual house to be bought, or viewing a show house, or by just looking at the plans and specifications. In most cases the sale will be finally agreed after construction, but it could take place prior to construction.

The second main approach to building is a contract to build. The essential features of this is that a contract must precede construction, and the building takes place on land owned by the client.

This book is mainly concerned with the second of these two approaches. There are two main variants to this second approach. The first is where one firm is employed to design and build the building. The second is where the client's designer is responsible for the design, and a separate contractor is employed to construct a building to this design. This book is mainly concerned with the second of these two variants.

1.6 Technical terms

In order to gain knowledge of a subject it is necessary to become familiar with the language of that subject. As far as possible, the various words and phrases forming the language of the subject of architectural design procedures will be explained, as they occur for the first time in this book. However, it is considered useful to provide a summary for easy reference, and this has been provided in Chapter 14. Readers are advised to refer to this chapter whenever they come across an unfamiliar word or expression.

2

Background to architectural practices

2.1 Introduction

This chapter explains how architecture emerged as a separate profession; how architects are educated and derive their authority. It goes on to examine the various types of architectural firms, outlining their method of operation including a consideration of communication within the design team and the relationship between architect and client.

2.2 The historic role of the architect

The word 'architect' comes from the Greek word 'archikton' meaning 'chief craftsman'. During the Middle Ages (about 1000 to 1400AD) the term 'architect' was seldom used. He was commonly referred to as 'Master' in English, 'Magister' in Latin, and 'Maestro' in Italian. Whatever the title, the architect in those days was considered to be a chief craftsman or master builder and overseer of works. He would not only plan and design, but engage the craftsmen and labourers needed to build his creations and also supervise the actual building operations.

It is arguable that by using the term 'chief craftsman', the person who controls the erection of any structure is an architect. Under this definition a properly erected wigwam, a primitive hut and Stonehenge are all the work of architects. Nowadays however, most critics would tend to argue that an architect is a person responsible for a building which is, not only conveniently planned and properly built, but is pleasurable to the eye of the beholder. This is summed up in Sir Henry Wooton's book 'The Elements of Architecture', 1624, of 'commodity, firmness and delight', which remains today as the standard by which many judge architecture.

In Egyptian times it was difficult to build structures which met Wooton's criteria. The slave labour used at that time was unskilled, and the buildings tended to be massively formed from huge blocks of stone. The best example is the pyramids which are still standing today. These pyramids were in fact huge royal tombs, and clearly the orginators of these gigantic structures possessed great mathematical skills. Surrounding the pyramids were colleges and temples. The temples were commonly constructed of granite, with tapering walls, rather squat pillars, and flat roofs. These Egyptian architects were proving that one of the simplest ways of roofing over a

Fig. 2.1 Greek architecture

building is to span beams from wall to wall, supported by pillars where required. Outside the more important temples there would be gardens, and at the entrance to the temple a pair of tall tapering shafts, square on plan and known as obelisks.

When the Greeks came to power the columns and beams used by the Egyptians in their temples were still employed. The Greeks however were essentially artists, and their apparently simple, though in reality extremely sophisticated buildings, such as the Parthenon in Athens, (see Fig. 2.1) were often used as a background to their sculpture. In Greek buildings all was not as it appeared to be. The columns were not vertical, but curved to give an illusion of straightness. Students of this period of architecture confirm that Greek architects, among other things had a wonderful sense of proportion and great mathematical skills.

The practice of architecture continued during the period of the Roman Empire, although the Romans lacked the Greek's artistic skills. The Greeks had understood the arch, but it was the Romans who used the arch freely, and this was one of the main contributions of the architects of the Roman period (see Fig. 2.2). They also devoted themselves to work which today we would classify as civil engineering, such as roads and fortifications.

With the rise of Christianity came a demand for a new type of building. There was a succession of styles. The Norman style was of heavy construction and very formal. It has been claimed that the man in charge of such a building – who we can call the 'architect' – was sometimes inclined to be a 'jerry builder', because rubble was often used behind the finely finished surface work. The workmanship improved with the coming of the pointed arch during the Gothic period from the 12th to 16th century. This period included the Early English, decorated and perpendicular styles (see Figures 2.3, 2.4 and 2.5). The stone masons themselves greatly influenced the detail of the final buildings, and it is not certain where the master's work ended and the mason's work began. In any event much more was left to the craftsmen than in previous times. Painters and poets of this period are well known to us, but much less is known of the 'architect' or 'master'. Examples are that the architect of Salisbury Cathedral is only

Fig. 2.2 Roman architecture

known to us as Master Robert, and the architect of Westminster Abbey is just known to us as Master Henry. Many great churches were supposedly designed and built by monks and priests, but whether they had architects or master craftsmen helping them is not known. Some masters were laymen, and very influential too, occupying important positions such as members of parliament.

During the Renaissance period, from about the 15th to the 18th century, England produced two of its greatest architects – Indigo Jones and Christopher Wren. Indigo Jones is sometimes referred to as the first architect, but he was also a celebrated theatrical designer and architectural draughtsman. He became surveyor general of the royal buildings. Christopher Wren was an architect, scientist and mathematician. He, like many of his contemporaries, was very much involved with the technology and structural theory of buildings, as well as the design. During this period, the architect, like the master builder before him, was a man of many skills. He would certainly be a builder and designer, but he might also be an artist, sculptor, scientist and mathematician.

It was around this time that the movement began, which was to see the establishment of civil engineering as a profession distinct from architecture. A corps of military engineers had already been formed in France when, in 1716, a body of civilian engineers was established for the building of roads and bridges. A similar development later took place in Britain, and by the second half of the 18th century, engineering was establishing itself as a separate profession, which was taking over many of the architect's traditional roles, particularly in matters relating to science. Early civil engineering concerned itself mainly with the building of canals and works associated with transport, but with the increasing use of machinery and the need for new structures such as mills, they extended their influence.

In some countries architects and engineers were considered to be a joint profession. Even in Britain there were those, like Telford, who reckoned themselves to be architect–engineers. In the main however, architects concerned themselves with traditional materials, such as stone, brickwork, concrete and timber. It was left to the engineers to involve themselves with the newer materials of wrought iron and structural steel. These materials were first used in mills, and then in the great railway stations, and were largely the work of engineers. It was the engineers too who were the most eager to use their scientific skills to make the best use of reinforced concrete and calculated designs, as opposed to 'rules of thumb' for timber and masonry structures.

Architects for their part were often engrossed in the artistic side of their profession, and frequently continued to hide their buildings behind a veneer of classical detail, so that by the Victorian era the architect was generally more concerned with decoration,

Fig. 2.3 Early English architecture

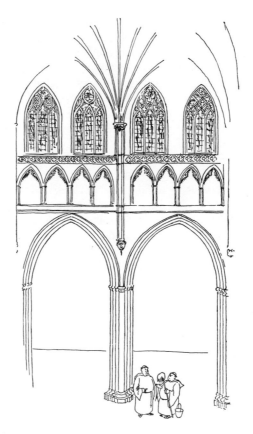

Fig. 2.4 Decorated architecture

while structure was the province of the engineer. Some buildings however, were the work of people who were neither architects or engineers. An example is the Crystal Palace designed for the Great Exhibition of 1851. It was the work of a gardener, Joseph Paxton, based on his previous experience of greenhouse design, and was adopted by engineers with great success in the design of railway stations previously referred to.

In the 18th century, as well as producing buildings for clients, architects sometimes erected building on 'spec'. By the 19th century, builders had separated from architects, and in the 20th century builders occasionally employed architects to prepare plans of their speculative housing and industrial schemes. Meanwhile, as buildings became more complicated, with a wider variety of components, materials and services, architects handed over more of their functions to other specialists such as mechanical and electrical engineers and quantity surveyors.

In conclusion, it can be said that the constant role of the architect through the centuries has been to plan or design buildings, including the production of many of the drawings required. Generally he has been, involved to some extent in the construction, either actually building, or being engaged in the supervision or inspection of the work. As has been suggested earlier, his detailed role has varied from period to period, and his skills have included those of artist, mathematician and engineer. At the present time we have moved away from the concept of the architect being responsible for everything, to a situation of shared responsibility. However, even though much of his original role has been taken over by others, the aim remains of producing a building which meets Sir Henry Wooton's criteria of 'commodity, firmness and delight'.

Fig. 2.5 Perpendicular architecture

2.3 Design team framework today

As has been previously mentioned, construction work, which of course includes the design, is more complex today due to a wider choice of materials and techniques, an increase in the scope of work, and the fact that jobs are more likely to be unique. This leads to the need for a properly structured design team in which everyone contributes their own particular skills. The architect has the task of designing the building as well as maintaining overall control of the project. The architect will, depending on the size of the job, have help from other architects and technicians. Sometimes they will develop their own specialisations and concentrate on particular aspects. For example one might prepare the perspective; another the schedules; a third the small scale location drawings; another might concentrate on more complicated areas of construction and, so on.

Apart from work undertaken by architectural staff, help will often be required from consultants for specialised areas of work. The RIBA Architect's Jobbook lists the following consultants services: quantity surveying, structural engineering, mechanical engineering, electrical engineering, landscape and garden design, civil engineering, town planning, furniture design, graphic design, industrial design and interior design. Sometimes these consultants' services are provided within the architect's own office by partners, associates, or directly employed staff. Sometimes the services will be by consultants in association with the architects. Frequently they will be undertaken by consultants in independent professional practices.

Whether or not it is necessary to employ consultants depends on the complexity of the project. For example if the project consists of a single house, the architect would consider the design of the structure part of his normal duties. If it were a large office block with a steel or reinforced concrete structure, a structural engineer would generally be engaged, and the client would normally pay additional fees for his services.

The most commonly employed consultants are probably quantity surveyors, structural engineers, and building services engineers responsible for mechanical and electrical engineering services.

The term 'consultant' is sometimes also used to describe persons, generally retired senior partners/directors, associated with architectural firms, to give advice as and when required. Throughout the project the quantity surveyor will be involved with the financial aspects, including the monitoring of costs.

The structural engineers will obviously be responsible for the main building structure. Often there will be a division of duties within the structural work. As well as the division between the designers and detailers/draughtspersons, there will often be specialisation between reinforced concrete work, structural steelwork, structural timber work, structural masonry etc.

A similar situation will prevail in the building engineering services section. Again there will often be designers and draughtspersons, specialising on electrical, heating and air conditioning, plumbing and drainage, fire protection work etc.

The design team will consist of architectural staff, together with staff responsible for the specialised areas of work mentioned above. The architect will generally be the co-ordinator of the whole of the project, instructing the consultants and having regular and frequent contact with them.

As, on a large project, many people are involved, the system becomes quite complex, and it is important that all activities are properly controlled and integrated. It is also vital to define clearly who is responsible for what; to allocate realistic time scales to each operation, and to make sure everyone knows what is happening.

2.4 Education of architects

As has already been mentioned, throughout the years there have been differing opinions as to whether everyone controlling the erection of a structure should be entitled to use the title of 'architect', or whether this term should be reserved for one who bears the responsibility for a building which, in Sir Henry Wooton's words, combines 'commodity, firmness and delight'. It was only during the 20th century that there was a successful attempt to restrict the architect's title.

It began in 1831 with the founding of the Architectural Society, who intended to establish a school of architecture to educate prospective architects. No formal examinations were set by the Architectural Society, but a condition of membership was that applicants had to complete five years of study.

In 1834 the Institute of British Architects (IBA) was formed. After only three years they were granted a Royal Charter, and changed their name to the Royal Institute of British Architects (RIBA). Since that time the RIBA has been the recognised head of the architectural profession in the UK. In 1841 Chairs of Architecture were established in Kings College, London. Students successfully completing these courses were awarded a diploma.

In 1847 The Architectural Association (AA) was founded, and eventually enjoyed Royal patronage. Its chief function was educational, and membership was open to all those engaged in the architectural profession. The AA asked the RIBA to establish an examination, and the RIBA did so in 1863. By the early 1880s the normal entry to RIBA membership was by means of examination. During 1887 the RIBA instituted an examination system of preliminary, intermediate and final examinations which were to last for 80 years, and be the forerunner of the present examination system.

In the 1880s the normal method of entry to the architectural profession was by means of training as an articled pupil in an architect's office. At later periods this was supplemented by attendance at evening classes and lectures. The success or otherwise of the training depended to a large extent on the choice of office.

In 1889 the AA set up their own examination based on full-time education, with studio instruction. Other full-time courses at various colleges and universities followed. These received recognition by the RIBA as giving exemption from the RIBA's own examinations, so that by the early 1930s there were 19 recognised courses. In effect the RIBA settled the question as to whether it was best to be trained in an architectural school or an architect's office. Its recognition and encouragement of such full-time schools of architecture had indicated its preference for school training.

Today a minority of aspiring architects continue to work full- time in architects' offices and study part-time for the RIBA's own external examinations. The vast majority however study full-time at approved schools of architecture in polytechnics and universities and are granted full exemption from the RIBA's examinations.

A typical course will be a three-year degree course giving RIBA part I exemption, followed by a three year post-graduate diploma course, with the first year being spent in a professional office, and with exemption from the RIBA's part II examinations. A further year of practical training follows, with an examination giving exemption from the RIBA's part III examination. The student is then able to register as an architect and become a full member of the RIBA.

2.5 Architects' registration acts

Once the formal examination system for architects was firmly established, the moves to protect the title of 'architect' began. At the time the issue was raised there were differences of opinions as to the motives of those seeking such protection. Nevertheless Parliament decided it was in the public interest to protect the architect's title, and ensure that all who called themselves architects were suitably qualified.

The Architect's (Registration) Act 1931 established the Architect's Registration Council UK (ARCUK) which set up a register of architects. Once established, the only new admissions to the register were those who had passed the RIBA recognised examinations. The title 'registered architect' was therefore protected.

The Architect's (Registration) Act 1938 extended the powers of the 1931 Act by restricting the use of the title 'architect' to registered architects. It is still possible for people to call themselves landscape architects or naval architects. Various titles are used today by people who, at least in part, undertake the work of architects although they are not registered, such as architectural designer, architectural consultant, architectural surveyor, and building designer.

In order to escape prosecution under the 1938 Architect's Registration Act, it is no argument to claim that you have the skills of an architect. The question is whether or not your name is entered on the ARCUK Register of Architects. In 1988 a case came before a magistrates court, where the ARCUK prosecuted a multi-disciplinary small works company for describing themselves as architects on their headed notepaper, despite the fact that they did not employ any registered architects. The firm was headed by a man who had qualified as an architect, and at one time had been on the register of architects. He had however ceased paying his annual fees to the ARCUK, and had therefore been struck off the register. He was convicted by the court and fined £500.

2.6 Architectural technicians

Many architects' offices employ, and are assisted by staff known as architectural technicians. In some cases such technicians are partners in architectural practices. Their role as stated by the Business and Technician Education Council (BTEC) is, 'to interpret, collate and present design information and develop it in the form of contract information for use by the construction sector; collaborate with, and take instruction from, the architect on the design requirements for a project'.

The professional organisation for architectural technicians is the British Institute of Architectural Technicians (BIAT). A member of their staff, David Wood, writing in the (BIAT) 1988 Yearbook, provides further clarification of the role of the architectural technician:

> The architectural technician is principally an architectural technical communicator, forging the link between architectural theory and construction practice. By interpreting the design concepts of the architect into detailed and practical building solutions, the technician forms the link between theory and practice. The technician's role is therefore, complementary to that of the architect, his main overriding concern being the sound technical performance of the building.
>
> In reality, the influence of a technician in any particular project is related to his or her qualifications and experience. Typically, the sphere of a technician's work tends to be varied and has been developing rapidly over the last few years.

It may include among other things:

Collection and analysis of technical data.

Preparation of feasibility studies.

Site and building surveying.

Design presentation.

Production drawing and construction detailing.

Application of computer-aided design techniques.

Materials selection and specification.

Environmental, structural and services design.

Design team liaison.

Cost control and tendering procedures.

Project and contract administration.

Site inspection and quality control.

Analysis of the performance of buildings in use.

Exactly what the architectural technician does may vary from office to office. In many practices the architect is responsible for overall design and management of a project, whereas the technician's task is to ensure the provision of good technical information and day to day site liaison. This is perhaps the most logical division of responsibility, but in some instances architects and technicians are to be found working side by side, performing identical roles.

The Society of Architectural and Associated Technicians was founded in 1965 and changed its name to BIAT in 1986. It is an associated society of the RIBA. Associate membership is open to those working in appropriate offices, who have passed either the Higher National Certificate or Diploma (HNC/HND) or BTEC Higher Technician's Certificates or Diplomas, provided they have followed a programme appropriate for an architectural technician. Applicants for full membership must complete a log book recording their practical experience, and pass a practice examination.

2.7 Architect's role as the client's agent

Under Section 2 of the Architect's (Registration) Act 1938 an architect is defined as 'one who possesses with due regard to aesthetic as well as practical considerations, adequate skill and knowledge to enable him to originate, to design and plan, to arrange for and supervise the execution of such buildings, or other works calling for skill in design and planning as he might in the course of his business, reasonably be asked to carry out in respect of which he offers his services as a specialist'. This means that the architect must show the care, expertise and application expected of people practising this profession. It does not mean that there'll be no mistakes. Building projects are often complicated and unique. Even if an architect works competently, and takes the same reasonable care and application as any other experienced architect it is possible, due to a combination of unfortunate circumstances, for things to go wrong. However the architect is unlikely to be held responsible if reasonable care, skill and expertise have been used. This matter is discussed in Chapter 4.

The need for an architect to act as a skilled practitioner of his art is vital because he acts as the agent for his client, or employer as he is legally called. He is therefore subject to the law of agency, which is part of the law of contract.

The term 'agency' is used to describe the special relationship that exists when one party, the principal, (who in the case we are considering is the employer or the client) employs another party, called the agent, (in this case the architect) to act on his behalf. There are several classes of agency. The usual class for architects is 'special', and means they act for the employer (client) in the design and supervision of one particular building.

The architect–employer relationship is generally formalised by a 'memorandum of agreement' between them, which is signed by both parties. A special form has been prepared by the RIBA for this purpose 'for general use between a building owner (i.e. the employer) and the architect or firm of architects'.

The architect's duties include entering into contractual obligations with a third party (the contractor) on behalf of the employer. In carrying out his duties he is expected to use the care and skill which the employer can reasonably expect of an architect. When agreeing to become the employer's agent the architect will be well advised to satisfy himself that his interests will not be in conflict with his employer's interests. The employer for his part is legally liable for acts undertaken by his agent, the architect, if they are undertaken on his behalf. The architect has many duties and responsibilities as the employer's agent, but despite his involvement he is not personally liable for claims made against the employer, provided he has acted within the terms of his authority.

Unlike the situation in which an employer engages someone as a salaried employee and can dictate the manner in which the work is performed, in the case of an agent, the architect can carry out his duties in whatever way he considers most appropriate. Nevertheless there are limitations. He cannot, unbeknown to the employer, hand over his entire duties to someone else. This does not prevent him using the services of other people such as quantity surveyors, structural engineers, building services engineers and clerks of works to assist him. Indeed this is the normal procedure in a project, except small, simple ones.

An architect's power to act as the employer's agent is strictly limited by the terms of the 'memorandum of agreement'. In the initial stages he is generally just acting as a designer. However at some stage, particularly when he is permitted to seek tenders from contractors, he is working as the employer's agent and must take care to exercise his professional skill and act in the employer's interest.

Although the architect is the employer's agent, he cannot do as he pleases. During the contract period he cannot instruct the contractor to undertake work which will vary the contract conditions. It is the normal procedure always to make it clear that he is acting as an agent and to disclose the name of his employer. If in doubt the architect should always safeguard himself by obtaining the employer's approval for his intended actions.

The main complication arises when the building contract is signed between the employer and the contractor, and the architect is named in the contract. This gives him specific rights and duties, during and after construction, in respect of matters such as the giving of instructions and approvals, and nomination of people to supply materials and undertake part of the work. These matters will be discussed later. Although he will undertake all these duties as the employer's agent, the courts have recognised that he derives power from the building contract in an almost independent manner. If disagreements arise between the employer and contractor, this again does not mean he can do what he likes, but rather that he must dispense justice between the two parties in accordance with the express terms of the contract. He therefore has the dual, and difficult role of being both the employer's agent and an independent arbitrator.

2.8 Architect's duty to the public

Architects are expected to show a high standard of professional behaviour. These standards are set out in the RIBA Code of Professional Conduct, and are aimed, not only at maintaining the status and uprightness of architects, but also at looking after the interests of the public. To this end, they seek to ensure that architects are not faced with a conflict of interests, by regulating situations where architects involve themselves in activities such as land and property dealing, contracting and estate agency.

2.9 Architects in the EEC

Under a directive which came into operation in 1987 architects in a member country of the European Economic Community (EEC) became eligible for registration in any of the other member countries. If architects from countries outside the United Kingdom wish to be registered in the UK they have to produce their diplomas, final year drawings and dissertation to the Architect's Registration Council of the United Kingdom (ARCUK). They are also required to pay a fee and convince an interview panel of their competence to practise architecture in the UK.

The aim of the directive mentioned above was to bring all EEC architectural qualifications in line with each other so that architects are able to work in any part of the European Community, regardless of which country they obtained their qualification.

In 1992 EEC countries will become part of a single European market. In readiness for this event many proposals have been made which will have significant implications for architects and others working in the construction industry. As well as formalising the mutual recognition of professional qualifications, they provide for the harmonisation of things such as building contracts and building regulations.

2.10 Professional indemnity insurance

Professional indemnity insurance is very much a fact of professional life. This is because if things go wrong, and the architect is sued for negligence, he may face enormous claims for damages. The purpose of professional indemnity insurance is to provide protection against the financial consequences of such alleged negligence. Negligence is discussed in Chapter 4.

Some architects may be convinced they will never make a mistake, but they will still generally need professional indemnity insurance. This is because if they fight a case which they win it can still cost money, and they must also take account of the fact that they are liable for their employees' and partners' mistakes as well as their own. In any case an architect wishing to undertake work in the 'public sector' must be insured, as public commissions can only be placed with architects carrying a minimum cover of £250,000.

The scope of the claim that can be made against a professional adviser can include the cost of the mistake as well as the cost of remedying the mistake. In other words it can include the consequential loss – i.e. loss which the employer suffers as a consequence of the mistake.

The basic policy offered by the insurance company to the architect will vary from policy to policy. Typically it will be the payment of all sums which the insured (i.e. the architect) shall be legally liable for as direct result of his acts of negligence, but will not generally cover 'exgratia' payments to protect goodwill.

The period of cover given to the architect is generally for claims within the period of insurance, i.e. it relates to when a claim is made for negligence, not when the negligent act occurred. The procedure for notifying claims is for the architect to notify the insurer immediately a claim is made against him, or immediately he is aware of an occurrence which may give rise to a claim.

The most difficult question the architect has to decide is the amount of indemnity insurance required. The minimum cover of £250,000 has already been mentioned for those who wish to do public sector work. Apart from this consideration, architects are advised to obtain as much cover as they can afford bearing in mind inflation, the growth of their practice, the fact that people are more likely to sue nowadays, and that courts are more inclined to award large amounts of money to employers making claims.

Architects need to be aware of the fact that professional indemnity insurance, like most other legal matters, is complex and should be approached with care. In particular when taking out an insurance policy, architects need to know precisely what cover they are obtaining. This is illustrated by a case which came before the Court of Appeal in 1988. A firm of architects, practising as an unlimited company, were appointed to act for a housing association in the refurbishment of about 350 properties. There were 17 separate contracts of engagement between the architects and client for work to the properties.

The architects had an insurance policy to protect them against claims for negligence with a limit of indemnity of £250,000 for any one claim. There was an excess of £2,000 for each and every claim – in other words the architects would have to pay the first £2,000 of every claim themselves. Serious defects occurred in the houses, and the client sued the architects for negligence claiming they had not shown sufficient care and skill. It was claimed that the total cost of the repairs was likely to be about £5.7 million.

During the course of the case the issue arose as to what constituted a single claim. If there was a single claim covering all 350 properties, the limit of indemnity would be £250,000 less 17 × £2,000 of excesses – i.e. £216,000. If however there were 17 claims (i.e. one for each contract of engagement between architect and client) the limit of indemnity would be 17 × £250,000 less 17 × £2,000 of excesses – i.e. £4,216,000.

A further complication arose when the insurers made the architects an offer in full and final settlement of their claims under the insurance policy. The clients for their part did not want this settlement to take place, as they were afraid that if the architects did not have the financial resources of the insurance company behind them, they would be forced into bankruptcy. This would mean that they (the client) would not be able to obtain the damages awarded if, and when, they won the case. They therefore brought proceedings under the Third Parties (Rights Against Insurers) Act 1930, to prevent the insurers being released from their obligations. The ramifications of this and other cases is beyond the scope of this book, but helps to illustrate the complexity of professional indemnity insurance, and the care architects need to take in these matters.

Organisation and business side of architectural practices

3.1 Introduction

In order to run a successful architectural practice, an architect needs to have abilities in addition to that of a designer. The architect must be a good organiser and business person. This chapter is concerned with that aspect of work, in particular with the various modes of practice and how they could be organised; with the function of the various members of the design team; with the need for good communications, and how architects obtain work and are paid for what they do.

3.2 Types of practices

There are various modes of practice which may be used by architects and these are summarised below. The type of architectural practice adopted is important because of the legal and financial ramifications, which will affect employers, employees as well as clients. The available organisational forms include self-employed principals, partnerships, unlimited liability companies, limited liability companies, integrated practices, group practices, and consortia.

Self-employed principals
Many architectural practices start with one architect working on their own, possibly from their own home, with the first jobs coming through friends and relatives. If the work expands the architect will employ staff to assist her and probably move into office premises. Alternatively she may decide to enter into some form of association with other architects.

Partnerships
Partnership is the commonest form of architectural practice. Architects enter into partnerships because of the extra strength and flexibility such an arrangement brings. There is some truth in the saying that 'two heads are better than one', and most professionals will sometimes find a second opinion helpful. It is also useful to have a partner during holiday periods and times of sickness or personal problems. The range

of partnerships is considerable. It may vary from two life-long friends working together in a single office, to a practice having a dozen branches, twenty partners, a hundred associates and five hundred employees. However, increasingly the larger practices tend to be organised as limited liability companies.

Partnerships are governed by the Partnership Act of 1890. This states that a partnership is a relationship between persons carrying on a business in common with a view to profit. It is possible for a partnership to operate on a very informal basis, but regrettably disputes do arise so it is generally advisable to draw up a 'deed of partnership' between the parties. All partners may participate in the running of the business, and all partners are agents for each other in respect of the business activities. The number of partners is usually restricted to twenty. Partnerships are often collo-quially referred to as a 'firm', rather than a partnership, but there is no legal significance in this term. If they wish to call themselves anything other than the names of all the partners they must register the name under the Registration of Business Names Act 1916.

A partnership means a number of people – i.e. all the partners – are legally liable for the debts of the business, but liability continues to be unlimited, in the same way as it does with a self-employed principal. It is important for architects who in reality are working as self-employed principals, not to give others the impression that they are in partnership. This could happen in the case of two architects who work independently, but operate from a jointly owned office.

It is important, particularly in cases where there are senior and junior partners, that the deed of partnership should clearly state the proportion of capital to be provided by each partner, and how the profit will be divided among the partners. It is also important to state the grounds on which the partnership can be dissolved. These include death, retirement, bankruptcy, and incapacity.

Sometimes partnerships give senior staff the title of 'associates'. Use of such a title gives the staff status in the eyes of the 'firm' and business contacts, but no legal liability unless the title 'associate partner' is used.

Partnerships have to pay income tax on their profits, regardless as to whether they are distributed among the partners or left in the business.

Unlimited liability companies

Companies are mainly controlled by the companies acts of 1948 and 1967. An unlimited company can have up to fifty members. A member, or shareholder as they are known, can be compared generally to a partner in a partnership, particularly in respect of being liable to an unlimited degree for the company's debts.

The main difference with a partnership is that a company pays corporation tax at a fixed percentage rate on their net profits. The arrangement governing their financial position is quite complicated, and there is not necessarily any advantage to be gained. For these reasons it is not very common for architects to operate under an unlimited liability company.

Limited liability company

Fairly recent changes to the code of professional conduct now permits architects, and most other professionals, to practise under this form of organisation. The most important, and from the heading, the obvious difference between a limited liability company and an unlimited company is that, in the case of a limited company, the personal responsibility of the 'partners' (i.e. shareholders) is limited. The theory behind this situation is that a limited liability company has a separate legal personality from its owners. This means that if the company gets into debt, the personal assets of the owners cannot be claimed to help pay off these debts.

This is of great importance, when an architect is subject to a claim for damages for negligence. This matter was mentioned in Section 2.10 of Chapter 2 and is discussed further in Chapter 4. As liability for mistakes, and alleged mistakes, by architects, with resulting claims for liability, is a very real problem for architectural practices, it is likely there will be an increasing trend for architects to practise as limited companies. It can of course be argued that a client who feels an architectural firm is practising as a limited company so as to protect itself against claims for negligence, may lose confidence in that firm and decide to take its custom elsewhere.

Public limited company

Even more recently architects have been permitted to operate in the form of a public limited company. A public limited company (plc) has the advantage of being able to raise large amounts of money from investors, both large and small, and to transfer the shares from one investor to another through the stock exchange.

The listing of a company on the stock exchange is also useful because it makes it easier for the company to raise additional capital if it wishes to expand its activities. All the 'partners' in such a firm will be shareholders, although not all will necessarily be on the board of directors.

Integrated practice

An integrated practice is one where the partners come from a number of different professional disciplines. Within the firm there may be one or more architects, structural engineers, building services engineers, quantity surveyors, town planners, and landscape architects. Such a practice can operate as either a partnership or as one of the types of companies mentioned above. Such a practice is most useful on large complicated projects, as it means clients can deal with a single firm, but yet still benefit from the full range of professional skills.

Group practice

In a group practice a number of separate architectural firms combine together, so as to offer an improved service to their clients, but still retain their independence. The precise arrangements will vary from practice to practice. One possibility is for several partnerships to combine together so as to undertake a very large job. One of the group members will have to take responsibility for co-ordinating the work and accepting liability as far as the client is concerned. Another possibility is that firms in different parts of the country may combine together for their mutual advantage.

Consortia

Consortia group firms from a number of different professional disciplines together, but each firm retains its separate identity. An example would be when firms of architects, structural engineers and building services engineers all cooperate in the design and supervision of, say for example, a hospital.

Service companies

Before changes in the ARCUK codes permitted architects to practise as a limited liability company, some architects used a limited liability company to provide non-professional services, such as renting or owning office accommodation, furniture and cars, and employing non-technical staff such as secretarial and printing staff. There are sometimes financial advantages in forming service companies of this type.

3.3 Design and construct organisations

In the nineteenth century, as has been stated in Section 2.2 of Chapter 2, it had become common practice in this country for there to be a clear division of responsibility between the design and construction of a building.

In more recent years design and construction, or design and build organisations, have been set up in which the contractor receives a brief directly from the client and is employed to undertake both the design and construction work. Design and construct organisations employ their own architects, structural engineers, building services engineers, quantity surveyors and any other necessary specialists. They are able to involve the contracting staff in the design process in an attempt to achieve the most economic solution in terms of both time and money.

Work can be obtained on the basis of a negotiated price. In order to reassure the client that he is not being asked to pay an excessive price, some design and construct organisations recommend the client to employ their own professional quantity surveyor to monitor the costs. Sometimes a 'shared savings' form of contract will be employed, so that surplus profit above an agreed sum will be shared on a 50/50% basis, or on a 'split' more favourable to the client.

The alternative is for work to be won on a competitive basis. Each design and build contractor will prepare a design and price for a building, based on the client's brief. The disadvantage of such an approach is that it may be difficult to ensure that you are comparing 'like with like', and it will probably be more time-consuming, thus losing one of the main advantages claimed for the design and build system.

Some of the advantages and disadvantages for design and construct as opposed to the traditional arrangement are given below.

Advantages
(a) The client is able to deal with a single organisation, and often with a single person, thus avoiding divided responsibility, and the possibility of confusion.

(b) Communication between the builder and designer is improved, which helps them to be more aware of each other's problems, and thus arrive at a better solution.

(c) It is possible to improve the programme time.

Disadvantages

(a) The quality of the design may suffer as the organisation may be over concerned with speed and cost of construction, at the expense of the design

(b) The client does not have an independent advisor to look after his interests.

(c) If the work is won in competition, the client cannot be sure he is comparing schemes of the same quality, and if the work is negotiated he may be paying above the market rate for the job.

3.4 Develop and construct

A variation of the design and construct contract is the develop and construct method. In this system the client employs an independent architect to prepare a sketch design, illustrating the client's requirements in outline, and the contractor develops a detailed scheme and price. The successful contractor will then be responsible for all the detailed production drawings.

The advantages claimed for this approach is that the architect ensures the client gets what he wants, particularly in regard to the planning and appearance of the building, but the contractor is able to ensure the solution is economic and practical because he has helped to influence the method and details of the construction.

3.5 Organisational frameworks

Although the practice of architecture is at least in part an art, it is also a business. It therefore needs to be organised in an efficient way so that the maximum use is made of everyone working for the firm. This organisation takes place at two levels. First in the matter of the overall organisation, and secondly in the way individual projects are handled. Both of these levels involve the use of what is sometimes referred to as 'organisational frameworks'.

An operational framework is an arrangement where the total work load of the firm is divided among the staff. Some may be working on their own, but the majority will probably combine together in groups. If the operational framework is properly devised everyone will know precisely what he has to do; whom he controls; and to whom he is answerable.

The simplest framework is a shallow one (Fig. 3.1a) in which everyone is answerable to a single person. As the number of staff increases this becomes impracticable, so a deep framework may be used (Fig. 3.1b). Project leaders are introduced, who receive instruction from the principal of the firm, and then in turn direct the work of a group of assistants. The number of tiers could be further increased to provide a deeper structure. Also in the case of an architect's practice, there may be two or more 'principals' (i.e. partners or directors) of equal status, each controlling either a number of assistants or a number of project leaders. A further variation is, in effect, a combination of a shallow framework and a deep framework (Fig. 3.1c). The principal controls some people working on their own, as well as a number of project leaders, who in turn control further groups of people.

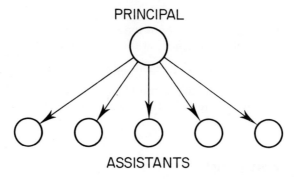

(a) Shallow framework

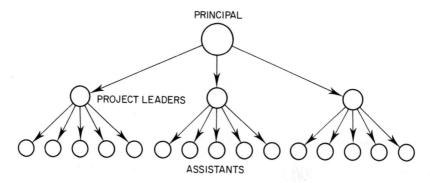

(b) Deep framework

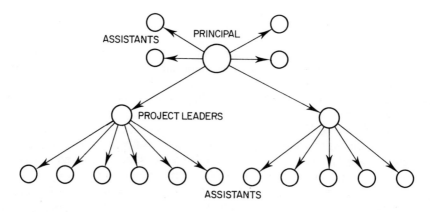

(c) Mixed framework

Fig. 3.1 Organisational structures

Reference has already been made to the two levels of organisation. In the matter of general organisation, an architectural firm has to decide the degree of specialisation they wish to pursue. If they are a fairly large firm, who employ staff with a wide range of experience, they may decide to make specific groups generally responsible for certain types of projects. One group might specialise in domestic work; another in commercial projects; a third in industrial projects, and so on. Alternatively there might be a design group responsible for all the projects in the early stages, and staffed with people who are particularly gifted in design and presentation work. They would then pass the project over to other groups when the production information stage is reached. In both the above arrangements a decision has to be made as to who is responsible for specialist areas of work, such as computer aided drawing and design, and non-technical matters such as administration.

In the organisation of an individual job, as mentioned previously in Section 2.3 of Chapter 2, there are decisions to be made as to how the various tasks are divided among the individual assistants. Assuming the project is a large one, undertaken by a group of assistants, the overall design would probably be mainly the work of the group leader, although one of the partners is also likely to be involved. Once the production information stage is reached a decision has to be made as to whether a degree of specialisation is introduced, or whether most people will undertake most of the different types of tasks. If the first model is followed, one or more assistants may be mainly responsible for the small scale location drawings; others might work mainly on assembly drawings; others on component drawings; with one or more assistants producing the schedules.

3.6 Some examples of organisational frameworks

Consideration will now be given as to the organisation of some typical architectural practices, and the implications on the people involved.

(a) The simplest situation is clearly that of one architect working on her own. She needs to make sure, only to accept work within her capacity to complete without assistance, and then to plan the work in as efficient a manner as possible.

(b) The second situation is almost as simple, and consists of an architect with one assistant. The architect will need to know as much as he can about the assistant's background, interests and ability, so that he can allocate tasks to him which he is able to do in a satisfactory manner.

(c) The next simplest case is shown in Fig. 3.2a. This indicates a shallow framework in which a single principal has a sufficiently small staff to be able to control them all individually. It is assumed that the firm undertakes mainly domestic work, with some commercial projects. Where possible, the five technical assistants specialise in one of these two areas. There is also a secretary who undertakes the administrative work, and an office junior, who does some of the simpler drawing jobs, but is mainly employed to run errands, file drawings and work the plan printer.

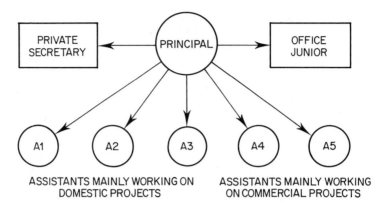

(a) Small firm with sole principal

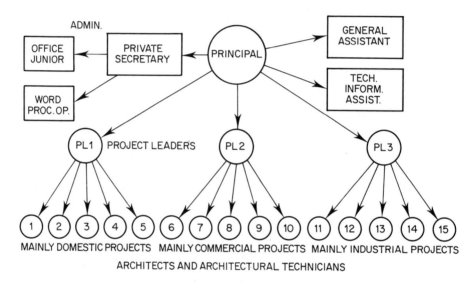

(b) Medium firm with sole principal

Fig. 3.2 Organisational structures of firms

(d) Figure 3.2b again shows a single principal, but this time as the firm is larger he employs three senior assistants whom he calls project leaders. These are either architects or senior architectural technicians, and they each lead a group of people responsible for one or more projects at any one time. The principal also directly controls a general assistant, a technical information assistant, and a private secretary who in turn controls two other assistants.

(e) As an architectural practice increases in size it may be best to introduce a further tier in the organisational framework. In the example shown in Fig. 3.2c it is assumed that there is still a single principal. Directly under him there are two associates, although in a firm of this size they may be made junior partners

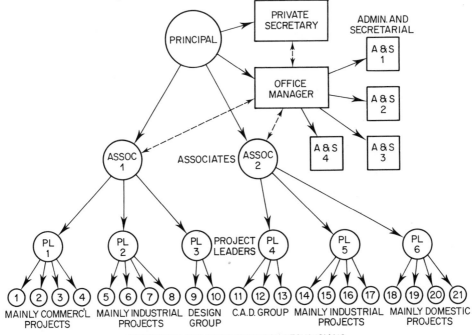

(c) Large firm with sole principal

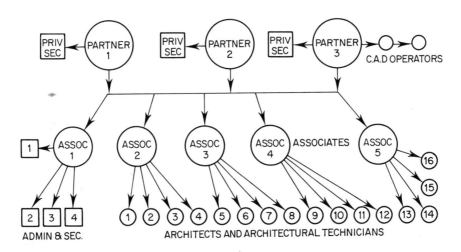

(d) Partnership

Fig. 3.2 *Cont'd*

instead. Both of these associates will control several project leaders, who in turn lead a number of assistants. The principal (or senior partner) directly controls his own private secretary, and also the office manager who is in charge of the administrative and support staff.

(f)   Figure 3.2d shows the arrangement for a firm in which there are three partners, who have five associates working under them. One of these associates has a special responsibility for the administrative side of the practice, and the others control one or more projects, under the overall guidance of one of the partners. Each associate has a team of assistants to help him. The partners each have a private secretary, and one of the partners controls the work of the CAD operators.

A similar arrangement to the last example could be followed in the case of a limited liability company, except that the title of director would be used instead of partner.

3.7 Organisation of individual projects

As well as achieving good overall organisation of the firm, the architect must also organise each individual project in such a way so as to enable the contractor to provide the client with what he wants, and also ensure that his own architectural firm makes a profit.

The organisation of a building project as it concerns the architect, is set out in considerable detail in the RIBA Plan of Work (see Section 8.2 of Chapter 8), but in general can be broken down into the following stages.

Deciding what has to be done
This is the thinking process. Tasks to be done include receiving the client's brief, organising the design team, preparing sketch plans and costing the scheme, preparing a full set of drawings and specifications, obtaining statutory approvals, preparing bills of quantities, selecting the contractor and sub-contractors, preparing the contract documents and administrating the contract.

Programming the work
This will involve setting a time against each individual task, and deciding what resources need to be allocated to achieve the required programme.

Organising the work
This will consist of allocating people to each task, deciding exactly 'who does what' and the manner in which they operate.

Coordinating and controlling the work
This means setting up procedures to ensure that everyone is working towards a common aim, with no task left undone or duplicated. It also means ensuring there is a satisfactory chain of command, with everyone aware of who they are answerable to,

thus minimising the risk of disagreement between members of the team. It will also involve checking that progress is being maintained at the required rate, and that the job is keeping within the office budget.

Organising record procedures
Architectural practices will tend to follow standard procedures and will often be guided by the RIBA Plan of Work. The procedures will include the ways instructions and information are issued, and the keeping of records for drawings issued and received.

3.8 Local Authorities and similar offices

Many architects and technicians are employed by local and central government. They will have an organisational framework similar to private architectural practices, in as much as there will be different levels of responsibility. In a county council's architect's department, for example, there is likely to be a county architect and a deputy county architect at the top of the organisational framework, and under them two or more assistant county architects, each responsible for a major area of work. In the next lowest line of command there will be a number of principal assistants, each responsible for a specific area of work. One of these may be responsible for educational buildings, and another for social services buildings. Under the principal assistants there will be further levels of senior assistants, assistants and technicians. Local and central government offices may also employ permanent site staff such as clerk of works, maintenance inspectors and supervisors.

3.9 Division of responsibilities within the design team

The number of design team people involved in a project, and the division of responsibility will obviously vary from job to job. In a large industrial or commercial project for example, the roles of the various members of the design team might be as follows.

Partner of architectural practice
He accepts the appointment, receives client's brief, advises on the choice of, and briefs the quantity surveyor and specialist consultants. He is involved with the feasibility study and with the outline proposals and scheme design, and will possibly be directly responsible for the scheme design.

Job architect
He will be responsible for the architectural team and have total involvement with every aspect of the job from start to completion. A job architect will often contribute towards the outline proposals and scheme design, and will generally have overall responsibility for the detailed design and production information. Other duties include

obtaining approvals under building regulations and town planning, liaising with other members of the design team, attending site meetings, and supervision of the work on site.

Other architectural staff

They will undertake tasks suitable to their abilities. Some tend to contribute more to the preparation of the presentation drawings. Assistants who are qualified architects may be particularly involved with the design elements of the job, whilst technicians may be mainly involved with working drawings where a knowledge of construction technology is of particular importance.

Quantity surveying team

A partner in the firm of quantity surveyors, or a senior assistant will coordinate and direct the work of this section, and in particular will be involved in budget estimates, cost checks and development of the cost plan. The preparation of the bills of quantities is the chief job of the quantity surveying team. There are a number of separate operations in the preparation of this, and various members of the team will be responsible for different operations. One or more assistants may be involved just with the 'taking off' and others for the 'billing'. The measuring and valuations for interim and final certificates and variations will generally be left to one or more senior members of staff.

The consulting structural engineering team

A partner or senior assistant of the consulting structural engineers will coordinate and direct the work of this section of the design team, being particularly involved with the initial consultation with the architect and advising on a suitable design for the main building structure. Designers will calculate and prepare the design, and preparation of the working drawings and schedules will be left to the draughtspersons or detailers.

The consulting building engineering services team

The organisation of this part of the work will follow a similar pattern to that outlined for structural engineering.

3.10 Communications

Good communications – by which is meant successful imparting or exchange of information – between all those involved in the design process, is essential. This can be achieved by various techniques including speaking, writing, photography, and models. Some requirements of good communications are as follows.

(a) A pleasant atmosphere is required between all the people involved. This calls for tact, understanding and consideration on everyone's part. If morale is low, and there are bad personal relationships it will be difficult to achieve good communications.

(b) Good leadership is necessary to inspire confidence, and encourage every member to perform to the full extent of their capabilities.

(c) Everyone should know how the office or offices involved in the design process operate, including the manner in which instructions and information are given. Procedures, such as always confirming verbal information in writing, and a standardised way of writing reports, should be strictly adhered to.

(d) Everyone's role should be clearly established, including status, in the sense of 'who is answerable to whom'.

(e) As far as possible every person involved in a matter should be given the opportunity to participate.

(f) People at the top of the hierarchy must pass information on to those under their control. People at the intermediate and lower levels must pass information sideways and downwards.

(g) Information should be given in a way suited to the background, knowledge and attitudes of the recipients.

When giving information to others it is useful to ask yourself a few questions. For example:

(a) Am I certain I have provided all the information required?

(b) Has all the information I have provided been factually correct, as opposed to being a mixture of facts and opinions?

(c) Have I given the information in the correct form? If in doubt give it in writing. This does not necessarily mean a formal memo – it can mean sending a friendly hand-written note.

(d) Am I sure the recipient will understand the information? If not, have I taken steps to remedy this?

(e) Have I made it clear as to the reason for passing on the information? For example, is the recipient expected to take action?

(f) Have I made it clear whether the recipient needs to pass on the information to anyone else, or seek the help of someone else? If so, does the recipient have the authority to get the help he needs?

If you have people working under you, it is important to be in control of the communication between members of your staff. Ensure that everyone knows the extent of their responsibilities and authority. This will help them decide what to do with information supplied to them, and whom to turn to for help. It is important that people know what they may, or may not do.

3.11 Telephone communications

Telephone communications can be the cause of strained relationships, and some clients have been antagonised unnecessarily by being left uncared for at the end of a telephone line. A few guidelines are listed below to encourage better telephone communications.

(a) Make sure you have enough telephone lines to cater for the volume of calls expected.

(b) Employ a competent telephone operator or other member of staff to answer calls.

(c) Answer calls promptly and pleasantly.

(d) If the person the caller wishes to talk to is not immediately available, he should, if possible, be connected to an acceptable substitute. Otherwise he should be given a return call at the earliest opportunity.

(e) Keep telephone calls as brief as possible, without appearing curt.

(f) Keep a note of all telephone conversations, particularly when information is exchanged, or decisions made.

3.12 Written communications

Care also needs to be taken when communicating by letters and memos. Again there are various principles worth following, and some of these are set out below.

(a) decide what you want to say, and then say it in a brief, clear and orderly manner.

(b) A good rule is to write as you would speak, if you had time to think before you spoke. For example, it is better to write 'thank you for your letter', than 'I acknowledge receipt of your written communication'.

(c) Write in a way the reader will understand. This means avoiding the use of technical terms to someone – such as a client – who has no technical knowledge.

(d) Avoid slang, and words which do not have dictionary definitions.

(e) Devote separate paragraphs to each item you are dealing with.

3.13. Fees

Although architects and technicians may not have entered the profession primarily to become rich, like everyone else they need money to live. They will therefore nearly always charge fees for their services.

The RIBA publishes a scale of recommended fees, but these are not mandatory. In most cases fees are charged as a percentage on the total construction cost. The fee system takes account of the complexity of the building, as well as the cost. Buildings are classified from classes 1 to 5, with 1 being the simplest. The full list is as follows:

Class 1
Industrial: storage sheds.
Agricultural: barns, sheds, stables.
Commercial: speculative shops, single storey car parks.

Class 2

Industrial: speculative factories and warehouses, assembly and machine workshops, transport garages.

Agricultural: animal breeding units.

Commercial: speculative offices, multi-storey car parks.

Community: community halls.

Residential: dormitory hostels.

Class 3

Industrial: purpose built factories and warehouses, garages/showrooms.

Commercial: supermarkets, banks, purpose built offices.

Community: community centres, branch libraries, ambulance and fire stations, bus stations, police stations, prisons, postal and broadcasting buildings.

Residential: estate housing, sheltered housing.

Education: primary/nursery/first schools.

Recreation: sports centres, squash courts, swimming pools.

Medical social services: clinics, homes for the elderly.

Class 4

Commercial: departmental stores, shopping centres, food processing units, breweries, telecommunication and computer accommodation.

Community: civic centres, churches and crematoria, concert halls, specialist libraries, museums, art galleries, magistrates/county/sheriff courts.

Residential: parsonages/manses, hotels.

Education: other schools including middle and secondary, university complexes.

Medical social services: health centres, accommodation for the disabled, general hospital complexes, surgeries.

Class 5

Commercial: high risk research and production buildings, recording studios.

Community: theatres, opera houses, crown/high courts.

Residential: houses for individual clients.

Education: university laboratories.

Medical social services: teaching hospitals, hospital laboratories, dental surgeries.

The scale of fees for 'new works' ranges from 4.75% to 10.5% and for 'works to existing buildings' from 7.25% to 15.75%. Fees may also be charged on a time charge basis – i.e. so much per hour, or as a lump sum fee.

Fees are paid at intervals based on the stages of the RIBA Plan of work, as follows.

Work stage C	15% of total fees due
Work stage D	20%of total fees due
Work stage E	20% of total fees due
Work stage F and G	20% of total fees due
Work stage H, J, K and L	25% of total fees due

VAT (see Section 3.14 below) at the current rate, is chargeable on the architect's fees and expenses. Quantity surveyors' and consultants' fees are charged additionally to the architect's fees, generally at rates recommended by their professional institutes.

3.14 Value added tax

People using the services of architects, or other people supplying goods or services, have to pay a tax known as a Value Added Tax – VAT. This is an extra percentage which is currently a 15% addition to the cost of the service – in this case the architect's fees.

It is not necessary to charge VAT if the turnover is below a certain figure, but most architects working full-time for themselves will normally earn enough in fees to make them responsible for collecting this tax for the government. They will need to be registered, and prepare three–monthly accounts in enough detail to show how much tax is payable.

3.15 Involvement of the client

The client is obviously the first person to be involved with the project, and his involvement continues throughout. Initially he considers the need to build, appoints the design team and briefs them. Then he approves the initial sketch design, provides whatever information is necessary for the more detailed design, and approves the architect's proposals. He provides further information to allow the detailed working drawings to be prepared and approves them where necessary. The contractor's tender then has to be approved by him, and he then signs the contract. During the building operations he continues to supply information as required by the design team. Throughout the project the client pays all the bills, and on completion accepts the finished building.

3.16 Influence of the client organisation

If the project is to proceed satisfactorily it is important to create a good relationship between the design team and the client. As a rule the design team will be required to match the client's organisational needs.

The first requirement is that the architect must keep the client fully informed of the progress of the project. This is fairly straightforward if the client is one person, such as a woman wanting a house built for her own occupation. Frequently however the client will be an organization, such as a private company, a public corporation, or a voluntary society. In these circumstances it is essential to decide precisely who, in the client's organisation, needs to be informed, and has the authority to issue instructions. Ideally this role will be restricted to one person, although he will invariably have a number of people to assist him.

Although the best arrangement is for one person to have authority to act for the design team, and one person to act for the client, in practice the design team will take account of the client's organisational requirements, and try to satisfy all his demands. This could mean that, on a large project, several people, in both the client's organisation and the design team are actively involved, but the key people should be made aware of, and possibly have to approve formally all decisions taken by their staff. In an industrial project for example, the factory manager may liaise with the project architect to agree the general factory layout; the plant manager may agree the services with the consulting building services engineer; details of the dock leveller may be agreed between the warehouse manager and an assistant architect; the client's accountant may agree the method of paying the accounts with the architect's office manager, and so on.

Large commercial organisations may have special departments, such as property or facilities departments, with the express function of briefing the architect, approving the design and issuing instructions. Employees in this department of the client's organisations may include architects, building and quantity surveyors, and others with some sort of building background.

Other private companies may appoint a person with technical expertise, even if not expressly related to building, to act for them in day to day decision making. An industrialist, requiring a factory built, may appoint the plant manager or production manager of his existing factory to this role.

A voluntary organisation such as a church or golf club, will probably have a committee to act for them, but it is best if the actual authority to approve the architect's suggestions is vested in one person, generally the chairperson. Often this person will be someone who has worked in, or has some knowledge of the construction industry.

A central or local government body, or public corporation, will invariably have an architect's department to fulfil the role of client, when they engage a private architectural practice to act for them. A county council for example, will often have an assistant county architect with the express role of liaising with private architects working for them.

A fairly common arrangement is for the appointment of the architect and approval of the basic brief, including budget costs, to be made by a very senior person in the client's organisation, such as the managing director, and then for all the detailed decisions to be left to some other person or persons.

3.17 Obtaining work

It is self-evident that, even the most brilliant architect will not succeed, unless he is able to obtain work, and successful architects are aware of the need to promote actively their architectural practices. Until fairly recently this has generally been done in a covert way, but with a changing 'climate' it is now openly acknowledged, even by the professional institutions, that effective marketing of architectural services is essential to success. Larger practices increasingly turn to public relations and advertising consultants, but even smaller firms need to consider how to sell themselves in the most effective way.

The first requirement is to be aware of exactly what you are able to offer potential clients, what type of jobs you are aiming for, and how to tempt clients to entrust their work to you. Various ways in which work may be obtained are as follows.

Traditional restricted advertising
At one time, the only advertising methods allowed to architects by the professional bodies, were to fix a name board of a specified size outside their office; or to write their name and title, again in a maximum size of letter, on the office window; or to

place their name under the appropriate heading in a classified edition of a telephone directory; or put their name on the site notice board.

Direct advertising

Direct advertising, albeit with limitations, is now permitted. This means, for example, that an architect commencing practice and interested in small domestic work, can display an advertisement in a local newspaper offering his services for alterations, extensions, and other types of work. It is also possible to produce brochures for handing to people or firms who may need the services of an architect.

Friends, relatives and social contacts

These are a useful source of work. The ability to make friends is clearly a useful asset in business, and can prove invaluable to architects starting up in practice. Whilst not many would freely admit to building up a circle of friends and acquaintances solely for business purposes, it is obvious that everyone is a potential source of work, and most people needing professional advice tend to think of someone they already know.

As a result of previous work

This is one of the most rewarding ways of obtaining work. A potential client may be impressed by a building he passes and seek out the architect involved to ask him to act for him too. If the building which arouses the initial interest is not completed, the name board which most architects place on the site of their building project, will obviously serve a valuable purpose in linking up the client and architect. If the building is completed, the potential client may approach the owner of the building for the name of the architect. Hopefully the architect will have enjoyed a good relationship with his client and the client will be happy to recommend him.

From other professionals

Work often comes to architects on the recommendation of other professionals, such as solicitors, accountants and bank managers. Sometimes architects will get to know such people due to social contacts. Some architects however, on commencing their architectural practice, make a point of visiting near neighbours of other professions to introduce themselves, and make their availability as widely known as possible.

Competitions

Taking part in competitions is the most difficult way of obtaining work, but is worth attempting, particularly when the subject of the competition appeals to the architect.

4

Architects and the law

4.1 Introduction

When an architect agrees to act for a client he is involved in a legal relationship with him. Among other things this could involve him in being sued for negligence. This and other matters relating to the legal position of the architect are dealt with in this chapter.

4.2 Negligence

An architect, like all other professional people, is expected to show a degree of competence appropriate to a skilled and experienced person. If he fails to do so, he may be faced with legal problems, notably being brought before the courts for negligence.

In this part of the book reference is made to important cases which have come before the courts. These cases must be viewed in a general way, as the rulings may be modified by the specific circumstances of other, apparently similar, cases. The law is a complicated business, and the intention here is merely to provide the reader with an introduction to the law of negligence, and other matters, as they affect the architect and his staff. If he is unfortunate enough to become involved in legal proceedings, the reader will need to seek the assistance of qualified lawyers.

4.3 Legal duties of the architect

Contract law
The duties of an architect is contractual because, generally before beginning work, the architect will make an agreement to act for the client. This Agreement of Appointment is a contractual arrangement. It will usually be in a written form, although in law there is no reason why a contract should not be purely a verbal agreement.

There are however certain principles governing contracts which can be summarised as follows.

(a) The parties to the contract must intend to make, and reach, a legally binding agreement. It is an important fact of contractual liability law that is based on consent between the parties to the contract.

(b) Under the contract each party must give something and receive something in return. The architect will generally give his expertise in the form of a design, drawings, specifications and advice, and in return will receive a sum of money from the client for these services.

(c) The parties must not be acting illegally, and the contract must not have been agreed under a misrepresentation.

Stamping of agreements

A written agreement can be 'made under seal' which requires it to have a 50p stamp impressed by the Inland Revenue within 30 days after it has been signed. Alternatively it can be unstamped.

Law of 'tort'

The architect's duties may also be imposed by the law of tort. It is not easy for the layperson to grasp the legal idea of 'tort'. The word 'tort' means a civil wrong, and the idea of the law of tort is to compensate a person who has been wronged by another. Unlike liability under contract law, which is essentially liability based on consent, law of tort is a liability imposed by the law.

4.4 Which law can the architect be sued under?

The architect, like other professionals, is liable to be sued for negligence either under contractual law, or the law of tort. Generally the plaintiff will claim under the law likely to provide him with the most favourable results, and will take account of factors such as time limits for claims, and the basis on which damages are likely to be awarded.

The Defective Premises Act of 1972 may also affect architects as a means by which they can be brought before the courts. This act relates to dwelling houses, and places on architects and others an additional duty to that imposed on them under contract law and the law of tort. It requires anyone who undertakes work relating to the provision of a dwelling, including conversion work, with the duty of ensuring that the work is done in a professional and workmanlike manner, so that the dwelling when completed is fit for habitation. An additional factor is that sometimes the architect, by acting in a negligent way, may also find himself liable under criminal law.

4.5 Definition of negligence with examples of court cases

Section 2 of the Architect's Registration Act of 1936 defines an architect as 'one who possesses with due regard to aesthetics as well as practical considerations, adequate skills and knowledge to enable him to originate, to develop and plan, to arrange and supervise the execution of such buildings and other works as he might in the course of his business reasonably be expected to carry out in respect of which he offers his services as a specialist'.

Glasgow University vs William Whitfield and John Laing Construction – 1988

This case concerned a claim by the university against the architects for negligence, as a result of their design for an art gallery built at the university. The university claimed that the architect's design was defective in the following areas:

(a) Dry linings resulting in condensation

(b) Roof parapets resulting in leaks

(c) Wood wool decking to the roof resulting in condensation

(d) Roof monitors resulting in condensation

In giving his ruling, the judge maintained that the architect owed duties towards the university, both in contract and tort, and that the standard of care owed was the standard of the ordinary competent architect using reasonable skill and care.

In the case of (a) part of the trouble arose because there was no provision for sealing the vapour barrier behind the dry lining at the edges and on the face. The judge held that, by the standards of 1976 (the date when the work was undertaken) such a seal was required and accordingly the architects were guilty of negligent design.

In the case of (b) the trouble arose because the felt roof covering was dressed up the parapet and tucked into a mastic sealed chase in the top of the parapet. Eventually the freezing and thawing action of the weather loosened the mastic seal and allowed water to penetrate. The judge held that by the standards of that time (1972–76) it was difficult to accept that the architect was negligent in his design.

In the case of (c) the judge ruled that while it would not be right to design the roof using woodwool in this way today, it could not be criticised by the standards appropriate to the time it was designed. Accordingly there was no negligence on the part of the architects.

In the case of (d) condensation dropped off the glass and metal windows of the roof monitors. The design was not a fully sealed double glazing system, but a cheaper system for use in industrial buildings. The judge held that the architects were negligent.

Most observers reading the full account of a court case such as the one referred to above, would probably feel that architects walk a tight rope in the matter of negligence.

D & F Estates vs The Church Commissioners – 1988

In 1963 the plaintiff, D & F Estates, were sold a luxury flat which was owned and built by the Church Commissioners through a joint venture company with Wates Ltd. In 1980 it was discovered that all the plasterwork was defective. Wates were held liable on the grounds that it was in breach of its duty 'to provide adequate and proper supervision of the plastering work'. The plaintiff was awarded damages in respect of the remedial work completed in 1980, with further sums in respect of future remedial work, and in respect of the loss of rent while the work was carried out.

However, later the House of Lords decided that none of this is recoverable as damages because a contractor is not responsible for the torts of an independent sub-contractor. Moreover remedial work necessary because of defects, or even potential dangers, is not recoverable as damages for negligence.

Warwick University vs YRM/Sir Robert McAlpine/Cementation Chemicals – 1988

This case involved a lengthy legal battle, which ended with a High Court ruling in 1988, and concerned the architects YRM, the contractors Sir Robert McAlpine, and the tile adhesive manufacturer Cementation Chemicals.

It was in respect of tiles which were fixed to the outside of a number of buildings at Warwick University. When it was found that water had got in behind the tiles, remedial work was carried out, which consisted of injecting an epoxy resin adhesive behind the tiles, causing some of the tiles to crack and fall off.

Both the architects and contractors were absolved from responsibility generally on the basis that they had followed the best advice available at the time. The judge said that in the 60s and early 70s when external tiled cladding was 'much in vogue' it was not generally appreciated that a weakness of the system was that ceramic tiling did not provide an impervious cladding. The judge stated that the university's expert had said there was no way in which the architect would have been aware of the risk. The adhesive manufacturers were however found liable for the massive repair bill involved. The judge stated that at the time the remedial work was carried out, Cementation Chemicals were the only UK firm licensed to use the epoxy resin techniques.

Presumably it can be assumed from this case that the architects were not liable because they had taken the same care that any other competent architect could be expected to take, whereas the tile adhesive manufacturers had been found liable because they had not taken the care expected from an expert in their field of expertise.

Sutcliffe vs Thackrah – 1974

The plaintiff appointed the defendants to design a house for him, and act as his architects and quantity surveyors. Building work began and the defendants, as part of their job, issued interim certificates to the builder, from time to time authorising payment to them for work they had done. Before the building of the house had been completed, the plaintiff terminated his employment of the builder and requested them to leave the site. Subsequently the builder went into liquidation. A second firm of builders was employed to complete the work.

The plaintiff claimed that the defendants had been guilty of negligence because they had certified work not done, or improperly done by the original builder, which meant in effect that the original builder had been overpaid. The House of Lords ruled that the defendants were liable in negligence for over certifying.

Walmsley Lewis vs Hardy – 1967

The plaintiff employed the defendant to survey a house for him, and as a result of the survey bought the house. The defendant noticed dormant dry rot but did not mention it to the plaintiff, and did not inspect the loft. The defendant later asked the plaintiff if he would like a further report with the carpets removed, and an examination of the loft. No mention was made of the dry rot, and the plaintiff decided he was satisfied with the original report. Subsequently the plaintiff had to sell the house at a loss.

The judge's ruling was that the defendant should have warned the plaintiff about the dormant dry rot, and was also negligent in not discovering extensive dry rot and damp.

4.6 Period of liability

Once it is decided there is a possibility that an architect, or other professional person, has been negligent, the question arises as to whether it is possible to sue that person, or if it is too late to take any action.

The general position is that in England, Wales and Northern Ireland the period of limitation – i.e. the period during which legal action can be taken – is six years, but twelve years for contracts made 'under seal'. The period of liability is unlimited where fraud is involved.

The next factor is, when does the period of six or twelve years commence from? Does it commence from the time the faulty work is done, or from the date when the faults caused by the negligence are discovered? For example, if the foundations of a building have been laid at the wrong level in the ground, the mistake may not be noticed when the work was done. The building might be completed and occupied by the client without any indication that some of the work was faulty. Then many years later settlement could take place, and serious faults develop in the building. If it were more than six years since the foundations were laid, the client would be unable to sue for negligence. It is even possible in the case of a large contract, built over a long period of time, for the limitation period for the foundations to end before the building was completed and handed over.

Many law cases have been concerned with the question as to when the period of liability for negligence dates from. The rulings do not always appear to be consistent, which leads to the conclusion that the situation has changed through the years. Some important cases are mentioned below.

Prior to 1977 it was generally accepted that the architect's liability was for a period of six or twelve years, depending on the type of contract. This seemed to change in 1977 when the Annis vs London Borough of Merton case suggested that the architect's liability could last practically forever. Fortunately for architects, later rulings qualified this situation.

Bagot vs Stevens Scanlon and Co. – 1966
The architects were sued for negligent supervision of defective drains. The judge ruled that they were not liable because more than six years had elapsed since the drains were constructed. At that time it was held that the Limitations Act 1939 provided for claims in ordinary contract or in tort being extinguished six years after the cause of the action occurred.

Dutton vs Bognor Regis UDC – 1972
The Council were sued for negligence because its building inspector had approved inadequate foundations on an infilled site. Lord Denning ruled that the six–year period

of limitation should begin from when the foundations were badly constructed, and not from when the defects were discovered. This meant that the plaintiff was unsuccessful in his action.

Sparham-Souter vs Town and Country Developments (Essex) Ltd. – 1976

In this case Lord Denning appeared to have changed his mind over the previously mentioned case. This case was also to do with foundation problems. Lord Denning stated: I have come to the conclusion that when the building work is badly done and is covered up, the cause of the action does not accrue, and time does not begin to run, until such time as the plaintiff discovers that it has done damage, or ought with reasonable diligence, to have discovered it. It may seem hard on the builder or council surveyor that he may find himself sued many years after he has left the work, but it would be harder on the householder that he should be without remedy, seeing that the surveyor passed the work and the builder covered it up and thus prevented it being discovered earlier.

Amis vs London Borough of Merton – 1977

Following a House of Lords decision in this case, which again was concerned with foundation problems, it appeared that architects, builders, inspectors and other professionals, would be liable for negligence for long periods after leaving the site.

The plaintiffs were owners of maisonettes which they bought fifteen years previously. In 1970 structural movement began to take place, which caused the walls to crack and the floors to slope. It was claimed that the foundations were not taken down as deeply as shown on the plans which Merton Council had approved. The Council were sued in 1972, more than six years from the time when the building was completed.

A unanimous House of Lords decided that the limitation period began to run when the defects first appeared in 1970. 'The cause of the action can only arise when the state of the building is such that there is present imminent danger to the health and safety of persons occupying it', said Lord Wilberforce.

D & F Estate vs The Church Commissioners – 1988

In this case, previoulsy referred to under Section 4.5, the House of Lords reversed a series of key court cases, including ones mentioned above. The ruling was, that under current legislation, the limitation for a breach of contract runs out six years from the date when the breach takes place – not when the damage was discovered, or should have been discovered.

Glasgow University vs William Whitfield and John Laing Construction – 1988

This case, also previously referred to in Section 4.5, threw some light on another interesting aspect of the law relating to negligence. In respect of the alleged design defect to the dry lining resulting in condensation, it was noted that the defect became apparent in the building after completion, and the architect gave advice on how to overcome the problem at that stage. It was ruled that when this happened 'the duty could be reactivated or revised'. The judge quoted from a ruling in a previous case: 'I am now satisfied that the architect's duty of design is a continuing one, and it seems to me that the subsequent discovery of a defect in the design, initially and justifiably thought to have been suitable, reactivated or revised the architect's duty in relation to design, and imposed upon them the duty to take such steps as were necessary to correct the results of that initially defective design'. This continuing duty was considered to be a duty both under the law of contract and the law of tort.

4.7 Persons to whom the architect may be liable

One of the rulings in the D & F Estate vs The Church Commissioners, 1988 case, previously referred to, was that architects and other professionals, are only liable to their clients under the terms of their engagement. In the current situation, architects are not generally liable to third parties, such as the future occupiers of the building.

4.8 Extent of liabilty for negligence

The D & F Estates vs The Church Commissioners, 1988 case, further resulted in the judgement that architects are not liable in tort for the cost of remedial work, as this is considered to be what is termed 'economic loss'. If the plasterwork was faulty and fell off the walls due to faulty supervision, the architect would not be liable to pay damages for the necessary remedial work. He would however be liable if, due to his negligent design or supervision, physical damage resulted to the plaintiff or his property.

4.9 Collateral warranties

Due to the fact that recent court decisions have tended to reduce the extent of the architect's liabilities for negligence, some clients are now trying to replace the third parties liabilities by asking architects to sign collateral warranties. These include the architect guaranteeing that the building he designs is fit for the purpose for which it is built, as well as assigning a warranty for future purchasers of the building.

Developers and large financial institutions are in a strong position to dictate such terms to architects. If an architect wishes to obtain a lucrative design contract he may have no option but to sign a collateral warranty on the client's terms first. However he puts himself in the dangerous position of increasing the area for which, if anything goes wrong, he can be sued for negligence. There is the added danger that the architect's professional indemnity insurance (discussed in Section 2.10 of Chapter 2) may not cover all the requirements of the collateral warranty.

4.10 Architects limiting their liability for negligence

Clients are not the only group of people anxious to protect their interests. In the past some architects have insisted that, as a condition of their engagement they limit their liability for negligence. However the Unfair Contract Terms Act of 1977 sets out to restrict exemption of liabilities clauses. This means, for example, that an architect is no longer able to say: 'I will act as your architect provided that if anything goes wrong my liability will be limited to £1000'. In particular this act provides a total ban on contractual terms aimed at excluding or restricting liability for death or personal injury.

4.11 Liability of architect partners

Partners in an architectural partnership are considered to be agents for each other in respect of the business of the partnership. They are therefore responsible for each other's business debts and torts, including such matters as the making of contracts, hiring and firing of staff, payments of money by the partnership, and for the damages awarded against the partnerhsip for negligence of the partners in the course of their business activities.

4.12 Liability of architect directors

It is now becoming increasingly common for architectural firms to operate as limited liability companies, rather than as partnerships. One effect of this is to change the liability for negligence of the architects involved.

A partner in an architectural firm who is successfully sued is personally liable for the full sum awarded against the firm, even if the negligence is due to the actions of his partner. This could mean him having to hand over his personal assets, including his home, to pay the debts of the partnership.

Architect directors of a firm practising as a limited liability company are less vulnerable. In law a limited liability company has a separate legal personality, quite distinct from its employees, including the directors. Up to now the law appears to adopt the position that the employees cannot be sued for the company's negligence. This does not necessarily rule out the possibility of a future claim against an architect director being successful. An aggrieved client might attempt to sue, jointly a limited liability company of architects and one or more of its directors, for tactical reasons.

However if such a situation were to arise architects might then try to persuade their clients to introduce a clause in the contract absolving the architect directors, or other employees, from personal liability for negligence proved against the company. The ultimate answer, apart from all architectural staff taking the utmost care in their work, lies in architects taking out sufficient indemnity insurance cover, although many firms are already finding this insurance an enormous burden on their financial resources.

4.13 Liability of employees of architects

An architect or technician employed by an architect in a salaried position is liable for his own torts – i.e. any civil wrongs he is responsible for. If the wrong act by the employee occurs during the course of his employment it is held to be the joint responsibility of the employer and employee.

The employee has a duty to take reasonable care in the way he does his work, as well as an obligation not to pass on confidential matters about his employer's business to third parties. This duty not to pass on such information to others still applies after an employee has left to take up employment with a different company.

4.14 Responsibility of architects for site safety

Generally, once a contractor takes over a building site, he is responsible for the safety of people working on, or visiting, the site. However, a case arose in 1987 when a firm of architects were charged with failing to provide a safe system of work on a site they were involved with. A member of the architect's staff, while making an unaccompanied visit to the site, fell to her death from the fourth floor, through a hole left by the removal of a staircase.

Previous to the case against the architects, the building contractor responsible for the site had admitted breaching the Health and Safety at Work Act of 1974, by failing to protect the hole and so prevent people falling through it. The Health and Safety Executive had stated there should have been scaffolding placed around the hole, or boards placed across it.

While accepting liability the building contractor stated that the architects had told him to leave the holes because they hadn't finished their survey and to fill in the holes would make the job more difficult. The magistrate concluded that site safety was not the architect's responsibility. 'It's up to builders to know the rules and to guard against accidents to their employees and other visitors', he said.

4.15 Copyright

Under the Copyright Act of 1956 'works of architecture' are included with 'artistic works' as being given protection against infringement of copyright. Works of architecture include models of the buildings as well as the actual buildings. Under another section of the Copyright Act (literary work) notes prepared by architects are also given protection.

The nature of copyright was defined as follows in the Gregory Committee on Copyright Law. 'Copyright is the right given to or derived from works, and not a right in novelty of ideas. It is based on the right of an author, artist or composer to prevent another person copying an original work, whether it is a book, picture or tune, which the originator has created. There is nothing in the notion of copyright to prevent a second person from producing an identical result (and himself enjoying a copyright in that work) provided it is arrived at by an independent process'.

In the case of buildings, the ownership of the copyright is vested with the architect who designed or drew the building. The important exception to this general rule is that if the design or drawing is done by an employee during periods when he is working for the employer, the copyright will be vested in the employer and not in the employee. Similarly if the design or drawing is produced by a partner, the copyright rests with the partnership and not solely with the individual partner who was responsible for the design. The copyright period lasts for fifty years after the death of the copyright holder, for example, the architect who designed the building.

4.16 Other legal matters affecting architects

There are also various other legal matters affecting architects which are dealt with elsewhere in this book. They are as follows:

Chapter 2
Restriction on the use of the description 'architect'.
The architect's role as the employer's agent.

Chapter 3
Legal ramifications of various types of practices.

Chapter 6
Obligations towards employees.
Obligations towards the general public.

Chapter 7
Legal constraints on design.

Chapter 9
Contractual responsibilities during the pre-contract period.

Chapter 11
Contractual responsibilities during the contract period.

5

Technical information

5.1 Introduction

This chapter explains the need architects have, of access to a wide range of information affecting the design and construction of buildings. It explains some of the ways that this information can be obtained, and the standard method of classifying information for building work.

5.2 Design and construction information generally

In order to be effective architects need the 'back-up' of accurate up–to–date information on design standards, materials, construction techniques, and legislation for buildings.

The sources of information to which architects need to refer include the following:

Manufacturer's and contractor's data on products and materials.

British Standard Specifications.

British Standard Codes of Practice.

Agreement Certificates.

Building Regulations.

Other Government legislation.

BRE publications.

Government leaflets and publications.

Contracts and other documents, particularly those published by professional institutes.

Technical articles.

Books.

5.3 Storage of design and construction information

The methods of storing design and construction information may take various forms. The traditional method is by manual storage, generally by means of shelves accommodating box files, lever arch files, or some other type of file. The majority of technical information prepared for such systems is produced to A4 size, though not everyone is willing to conform to this standard size.

Large offices may employ one or more technicians, or librarians, to set up and maintain their reference library. An alternative method is to engage an independent commercial organisation to undertake this work. Smaller offices may use a junior technician, or a non-technical member of the office staff to file information, but in this case a senior assistant will generally be responsible for selecting the material.

Although manual storage methods are still widely used, and should not be despised, it is becoming common practice for other methods, including sophisticated computer systems, to take their place. Such systems will vary from office to office, and in most cases will be updated and changed every few years. Students should welcome the opportunity to gain 'hands on' experience of such systems, as they generally enable information to be obtained with greater speed and less effort.

5.4 CI/SfB system

There are many filing systems which could be used for filing technical information about the construction industry, but the system in general use is known as the CI/SfB system. This is of Swedish origin, but was introduced into this country by the RIBA. Architectural staff need to be familiar with it, particularly those involved in the management of such a system. To achieve complete familiarity with CI/SfB it is important to study the CI/SfB Construction Indexing Manual produced by RIBA Publications Ltd. There is no adequate substitute for this procedure, but as an introduction, the main features of the system are summarised below.

Everything is classified under five tables.

Table 0 covers the physical environment. It concludes items such as planning areas, but is mainly concerned with different types of buildings or facilities. Each type of building or facility is given a distinctive number. For example:

6   denotes religious facilities generally.
61   denotes religious centre facilities.
62   denotes cathedrals.
63   denotes churches, chapels.
64   denotes mission halls, meeting houses.
65   denotes temples, mosques, synagogues.
66   denotes convents.
67   denotes funerary facilities, shrines.
68   denotes other religious facilities.

Table 1 deals with particular functions which combine to make up the facilities in Table 0. They include substructure items, such as foundations; primary elements, such as walls, floors and roofs; secondary elements, such as window/door openings and suspended ceilings; finishes, such as wall, floor and ceiling finishes; services, mainly piped and ducted; other services, mainly electrical; fittings, such as sanitary fittings; loose furniture; and external elements.

Each item is given a distinctive bracketed number. For example:

(2-) denotes primary structural elements.
(21) denotes external walls.
(22) denotes internal walls.
(23) denotes floors.
(24) denotes stairs.
(27) denotes roofs.
(28) denotes building frames.

Table 2 deals with constructions of forms which combine together, to make up the elements in Table 1. Each form is given a distinctive capital letter. For example,

F denotes blocks, blockwork, bricks, brickwork.
G denotes large blocks and panels.
H denotes sections such as structural steel sections.
I denotes pipework.

Table 3 deals with the materials which combine to form the products in Table 2. They include formed materials, such as clay to make bricks and metal to make sections; Formless materials such as concrete and mortars; and what are termed functional materials such as paint. Each category of material is given a lower case letter, and these main categories can be further sub-divided by use of a number added to the lower case letter. For example:

g denotes clay (dried, fired).
g1 denotes dried clay.
g2 denotes fired clay.
g3 denotes glazed fired clay.
g6 denotes refractory materials (e.g. fireclay).

Table 4 deals with activities which assist or affect construction, but are not incorporated in it. Each item is given a combined capital letter and number set within brackets. For example:

(K) denotes fire, explosion.
(K1) denotes sources, types.
(K2) denotes fire protection.
(K3) denotes fire resistance (structures).
(K4) denotes reaction to fire (materials).
(K5) denotes smoke etc.
(K6) denotes explosions.
(K7) denotes fire explosion damage, salvage.

Fig. 5.1 shows the general concept of the system in a diagramatic form. Fig. 5.2 shows how Tables 1, 2 and 3 are used.

Lists of the main subject headings for the five tables are given below. The sub-division of the various tables are equally important, and the reader will need to study the CI/SfB Construction Indexing Manual, published by RIBA Publications Ltd., for this information.

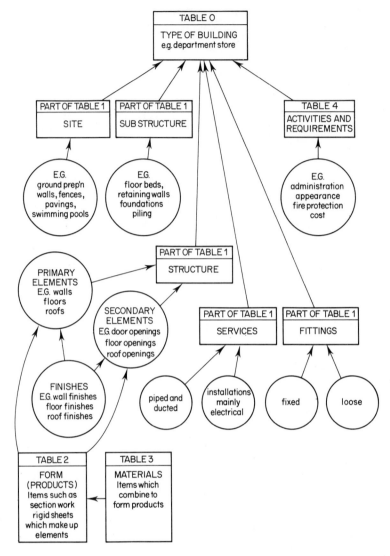

Fig. 5.1 General concept of SfB system for technical information

Table 0

    0 Planning areas.
    1 Utilities, civil engineering facilities.
    2 Industrial facilities.
    3 Administrative, commercial, protective service facilities.
    4 Health, welfare facilities.
    5 Recreational facilities.
    6 Religious facilities.
    7 Educational, scientific, information facilities.
    8 Residential facilities.
    9 Common facilities, other facilities.

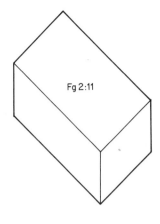

Fg 2:11

TABLE 1	TABLE 3	
F	g2	·11
DENOTES IT IS BRICKWORK	DENOTES THE BRICK IS FORMED OUT OF FIRED CLAY	DENOTES IT IS A SPECIFIC TYPE OF FIRED CLAY BRICK E.G. MANUFACTURED TO A PARTICULAR B.S.S.

(21.3) Fg 2·11

TABLE 1		TABLES 2&3
(21	·3)	Fg 2·11
EXTERNAL WALL	NON– LOAD BEARING	AS INDICATED ABOVE

Fig. 5.2 Use CI/SfB tables 1, 2 and 3

Table 1
(1-) Ground, substructure.
(2-) Structures, primary elements, carcass.
(3-) Secondary elements, completion of structure.
(4-) Finishes to structure.
(5-) Services, mainly piped, ducted.
(6-) Services, mainly electrical.
(7-) Fittings.
(8-) Loose furniture equipment.
(9-) External elements, other elements.

Table 2
A Construction forms.
B Vacant.
C Excavation and loose fillwork.
D Vacant.
E Cast *in situ* work.
F Blockwork, brickwork.
G Large blocks, panel work.
H Section work.
I Pipe work.
J Wire work.

K Quiltwork.
L Flexible sheet work (proofing).
M Malleable sheet work.
N Rigid sheet overlap work.
P Thick coating work.
R Rigid sheet work.
S Rigid tile work.
T Flexible sheet work.
U Vacant.
V Film coating and impregnation work.
W Planting work.
X Work with components.
Y Formless work.
Z Joints.

Table 3

e Natural stone.
f Precast with binder.
g Clay (dried, fired).
h Metal.
i Wood.
j Vegetable and animal materials.
k Vacant.
l Vacant.
m Inorganic fibres.
n Rubbers, plastics, etc.
o Glass.
p Aggregates, loose fills.
q Lime and cement binders, mortars, concrete.
r Clay, gypsum, magnesia and plastics binders, mortars.
s Bituminous materials.
t Fixing and jointing materials.
u Protective and process/property modifying materials.
v Paints.
w Ancillary materials.
x Vacant.
y Composite materials.
z Substances.

Table 4

(A) Administration, management, activities, aids.
(B) Construction plant, tools.
(C) Vacant.
(D) Construction operations.
(E) Composition etc.
(F) Shape, size etc.

(G) Appearance etc.
(H) Context environment.
(I) Vacant.
(J) Mechanics.
(K) Fire, explosion.
(L) Matter.
(M) Heat, cold.
(N) Light, dark.
(P) Sound, quiet.
(Q) Electricity, magnetism, radiation.
(R) Energy, other physical factors.
(S) Vacant.
(T) Application.
(U) Users, resources.
(V) Working factors.
(W) Operation, maintenance, factors.
(X) Change, movement, stability, factors.
(Z) Peripheral subjects, form of presentation, time, place.

5.5 RIBA products library data

Among the organisations offering information on building products and services is the RIBA Services Ltd. They produce A4 information sheets on various products, based on information supplied by the manufacturers. The format of the sheets are standardised, so making it easier to compare the different products. The sheets are assembled in a series of binders, which are regularly updated.

5.6 Microfile information system

One alternative to a manual information system using A4 pages is a microfile information system, such as the Barbour Technical and Product Microfile Systems. The information is produced on 'microfiche', which is the name given to a small sheet of film bearing a microphotograph – i.e. a photograph reduced to a very small size – of the document containing the required information.

The Barbour Technical Microfile uses a constantly updated reference library of over 6000 technical publications from government departments, research bodies, standards and professional institutions. The information covers design and construction, legislation, standards, codes, and building science. All this information is housed in a container about the size of a shoe box.

The Barbour Products Microfile provides manufacturer's information on their products, and is claimed to cover every known type of product used in the UK construction industry. The information is collected from about 1000 manufacturers for about 5000 different products.

The system is supplied with an index, which enables the desired microfiche to be selected. A 'reader' which is something like a t.v. screen, is also supplied. When the microfiche is placed in the reader the document can be read in its entirety. If required, a reader printer can be provided, which enables 'hard' (paper) copies to be obtained.

5.7 Computer information system

Another alternative is a computer information system. There are a number of firms which provide information on discs which can be fed into a computer system to provide a wide range of information, such as building regulations, BRE publications, and product details. The information is able to be regularly updated. It is displayed on a t.v. type screen, but paper copies can be obtained, as required, by means of a printer.

Increasingly access to this kind of information is obtained by use of telephone lines. The principle involved is to link a 't.v. set' in the office to a computer centre where all the required data is stored and relayed from the telephone exchange via the telephone lines.

5.8 Cost information generally

The cost aspect is the particular concern of the quantity surveyor, who will generally be employed as the client's financial advisor on all but the smallest projects. However many architects will maintain their own cost information.

The information may consist of a detailed build-up of building costs, based on labour and material rates plus preliminaries, overheads and profit, but will more likely take the form of approximate estimating information. Details of approximate estimating are given in Chapter 9. There are many sources of information for approximate estimating. Some comments on four sources are given below.

5.9 Cost analysis of previous jobs

Methods used, and the system of recording the information will vary from office to office. One method is to keep a loose leaf record book with one or more pages for each different type of building. As each job is completed, basic details, such as total floor area, total cost, and price per square metre of floor area, are recorded. A note is also made of any special circumstances which made the job more, or less expensive than average. To use this information as a guide for a new project, it is necessary to update the costs (generally by means of a percentage increase) to allow for the change which has taken place in building costs during the period between the two jobs.

This can be a useful method, particularly if the person using the information is familiar with both the earlier projects and the current one. However, care has to be taken in applying the correct percentage increase, and to take full account of local and national cost trends, and any special circumstances for a particular project.

5.10 Price books and journals

There are a number of excellent price books available which provide information, useful for preparing approximate estimates. The current Wessex price book, for example, is a two–volume edition of 2000 pages, and clearly contains much valuable information. However good the books are, they should be used with discretion, and some quantity surveyors would claim it is foolhardy to use them for anything other than 'back-up' information. A number of technical journals for architects and builders also provide similar information to that shown in price books.

5.11 Computer estimating systems

A number of firms provide software packages – i.e. disks – with information for feeding into computers. Most of these are comprehensive estimating packages providing thousands of prices of materials, components and labour costs, to enable detailed prices to be built up for contractors' tenders. However, many of them provide the sort of information the architect needs when calculating the approximate cost of a building project. The various systems are generally updated at regular intervals.

5.12 RICS building cost information service

The best known and most comprehensive cost information service is probably the RICS Cost Information Service. This offers cost information suitable for every stage of a building project from feasibility studies in the initial stage, to cost control during operations on site.

The service is based on the principle of reciprocity, and subscribers to the service undertake to provide data from their own sources, and in return to receive information made available by all. As a result they have a 'bank' of information available covering 5000 projects.

Included in the service are building price schedules, containing average £ per square metre prices, for over 300 building types. The coverage is exhaustive. For example, the section on factories covers 18 categories, such as different sizes and various methods of construction. The information is updated quarterly. There is also concise cost analyses containing data from a large number of projects, to give a range of prices for early cost estimating. The cost is broken down into the main elements of substructure, superstructure, internal finishes, fittings, services, external works and preliminaries.

Furthermore, there is a library of detailed cost analyses of actual projects, which can be used for budgeting and estimating, to produce probable costs of future projects. As the title suggests, these analyses are more detailed and break the cost down into each individual element. For example, the 'breakdown' of the superstructure includes items such as upper floors, roof, stairs, external walls, windows and external doors, and the services 'breakdown' includes items such as sanitary appliances, water installations, ventilating systems, electrical installations and gas installations.

5.13 Samples

Architects often maintain a collection of samples of various building products, such as bricks, tiles, ironmongery, flooring materials, glazed tiles and electrical accessories, both for use by their own staff and also for showing to clients.

It is important that these samples are labelled with information on the name and address of the supplier, the date they were obtained, and the cost. It is also important they are arranged in an orderly manner. Generally they will be on shelving. Larger firms may have a special samples room, or use part of their reference library for this purpose, but in smaller firms the sample shelves will be fixed in some convenient area of the office.

5.14 Record drawings

Even when a building is completed and handed over to the client, architects will still need to keep, and have access to, many of the drawings used for the construction of the project. This is because queries on the building's construction may arise at some time in the future. There may be extensions or alterations required to the building, or drawings of previously constructed buildings may be useful to the architect for one of his future jobs.

Generally only the negatives will be retained. These can be stored in metal tubes, and arranged on shelves or racks. They should of course be labelled, and if more than one tube is required for a particular project, it is best to strap them together.

This traditional method of filing record drawings has the disadvantage of using up space. If less desirable spaces, such as basement and attic areas, are available, they may become the home for record drawings. Otherwise valuable and expensive office space will be lost.

As an alternative to the traditional system, use may be made of a microfilm storage system. The original drawings, reproduced on A3, A2, A1 or A0 sheets are transferred onto 35mm microfilm copies, which can be conveniently filed in a relatively small cabinet. It has been estimated that microfilm copies only need about 5% of the space taken up by traditional drawings.

The microfilm copies need to be accurately indexed, but once this is done they are easily located and retrieved when needed. They have the further advantage of being able to be housed in a lockable, fire resistant container. Readers are available for viewing the microfilm copies, and printing can be arranged, or as printer–supplied by companies specialising in microfilming work.

6

General office practice

6.1 Introduction

As well as organising the technical side of their work, architects, like all other professional and business people need to attend to matters such as arranging accommodation, furnishings, and insurances. They also have obligations to the staff they employ, in respect of conditions of work, National Insurance, income tax and holidays. This chapter deals with such matters.

6.2 Accommodation

Architects will generally try to obtain the best possible accommodation which they can afford, so as to provide agreeable working conditions for their staff, and an inviting atmosphere for visitors, particularly clients. In practice they will be limited by what is available within their price range in the area where they wish to operate, and whether the available accommodation is for renting, leasing or for sale.

A reception/waiting area is a useful feature of an architect's office, although clients in particular do not expect to be kept waiting. Facilities will also be required within the office accommodation for meetings with clients and others. This space may be arranged within the partners/directors offices, although often a separate meeting room will be available.

Other areas will be required for both the architectural and other technical staff, and secretarial and administrative staff. A computer aided design and drawing system (CAD) will frequently be arranged in separate rooms or areas. Library and other storage space will generally be provided, together with toilets, and at least a small kitchen area for tea and coffee making.

6.3 Furniture

The standard of furniture will vary enormously, from fully carpeted and curtained offices, with attractive furniture, and internal landscaping, to the distinctly spartan or positively grotty.

Partners and directors will generally, as a minimum requirement, be provided with a desk, drawing facilities, possibly a plan chest, and enough chairs for themselves and their visitors.

Other architectural staff will require drawing facilities, chairs or stools, laying out space for drawings, catalogues etc., and facilities for storing drawings.

Secretarial and administrative staff will require desks, chairs, storage facilities for files and stationery, and typewriters and computer equipment. Computer equipment is discussed further in Section 6.10 of this chapter. Equipment for office staff will generally be in the office work areas.

6.4 Telephones

An adequate number of telephones is essential, with a phone located within easy reach of each worker, as even the most junior staff will occasionally have to take phone calls. People, including clients, can get very frustrated if due to too few lines being available they have difficulty in making contact with the architect and staff. Mention has already been made under Section 3.11 of Chapter 3, on the importance of a pleasant, competent telephone operator to create a good initial impression on callers.

6.5 Stationery

Architects setting up in practice will need to obtain a range of normal stationery items such as headed notepaper. They will also need to obtain a whole range of standard forms. These can be individually designed, but many architects will choose to use the standard forms designed by the RIBA or BIAT. Examples of such forms are included in Chapter 13.

6.6 Health, welfare and safety of employees

Whatever accommodation is provided the architect, as an employer of staff, is responsible for complying with the requirements of the Offices, Shops and Railway Premises Act of 1963, and the Health and Safety at Work Act of 1975. These include provision for the health, welfare and safety of people employed in offices.

Among the things the architect–employer, like all other employers of office staff, must provide are the following:

Fire precautions
A safe means of entering and leaving the building, and sufficient and suitable fire extinguishing equipment.

Lifts
Where these are provided they must be safe, state the maximum loads, and be examined by a competent person every six months.

Toilets
Enough suitable toilets, which are kept separate for each sex. For example 5 w.cs. for men and 5 w.cs. for women will be enough for up to 100 of each sex.

Washing facilities
Enough basins, with hot and cold water, soap and drying facilities must be provided, generally on the same scale as w.cs.

Drinking water
An adequate supply of drinking water must be provided.

Working space
Each worker is to have a minimum of 3.72 square metres (40 square feet) or 11.52 cubic metres (400 cubic feet) of space in his or her workroom.

Seating
Where work can be done sitting down, an appropriate seat with proper support must be provided for each worker.

Ventilation
An adequate supply of fresh or purified air must be provided.

Temperature
The premises must be heated to a reasonable temperature, generally to a minimum of 60° F.

Lighting
Enough suitable lights must be provided.

6.7 Insurance of premises and contents

If architects own their own office building, they will need to insure it against loss and damage due to fire, burglary, and other less likely mishaps, such as lightning, explosions, damage by aircraft, storms, floods and earthquakes.

In any event, they will need to take out insurance cover for the contents of their offices. The main thing is to ensure that the cover obtained is adequate to replace the full value of the loss and damage incurred. Most insurance companies offer indexed linked schemes which take account of the effects of inflation.

As well as the normal contents of the premises, architects also need to cover the cost of replacing drawings, specifications and other documents damaged or destroyed, including those documents in the course of preparation.

6.8 Employer's liability insurance

Architects, like other employers, need to take out insurance against claims made on them either by their employees, or by members of the public.

There is a legal responsibility placed on employers to take out insurance to cover claims arising out of injury or death of their employees. The premiums are based on the class of employee and the salary paid.

Insurance can, if desired, also be taken out to cover claims by members of the public against the employer, for example, a client who, when visiting the architect's office, slips on the floor and injures himself.

An employer is also liable for any wrong done by a member of his staff which occurs while the employee is engaged on his employer's business, and most employers will therefore insure themselves against such action by their employees. An employer is not however liable for a wrong done by an employee outside his normal course of employment.

6.9 Other insurances

Architect–employers, also need to take out other insurance policies, such as for company cars, travel insurance, insurance to cover special situations, such as the death of partners/directors, possible private health care insurance, and policies covering pensions for partners/directors and staff.

6.10 Use of computers

Like most other professions and groups of people, architects tend to show a mixed reaction to the use of computers, ranging from total commitment to this 'new tool', to a combination of distrust and fear. Increasingly they are becoming part of the teaching programme for architects and technicians – e.g. they are already an essential element of most BTEC programmes – so it is likely they will, in the future, have an increasing role to play in architects offices.

Computers are becoming more compact, able to work faster, and capable of storing huge amounts of information. A computer can take many forms, but commonly will consist of a central processor, a typewriter style of keyboard, and a visual display unit, similar to a t.v. screen. One job a computer can do is to supply information. Telephone links are now available to link contributors to a network of technical, scientific and legal information. They can also undertake their original role of calculators, although they are now able to solve far more complicated mathematical problems than were originally envisaged.

Computers can fulfil the function of an office filing system, using a fraction of the space required by a traditional filing system. They are also available to deal with routine office tasks, such as office accounts, payment of salaries, VAT etc.

Architects can, with the aid of a computer, have at their disposal, a mass of technical and design information which they can use to drive an electronic drawing board, displaying a pictorial representation of their designs.

However, computers are only as useful and reliable as the quality of the programmes written for them, and the quality of the staff operating them. Many programmes are available commercially for architects and others to buy. Some architectural practices employ their own staff to design and write their own programmes. Trained staff are also required to operate the computers.

Computer information systems are discussed in Section 5.7 of Chapter 5, and computer aided design and drawing systems in Section 8.9 of Chapter 8.

6.11 Employment of staff generally

Architects employing staff have certain legal responsibilities relating to matters such as contracts of employment, dismissal, redundancy, national insurance, and income tax.

6.12 Conditions of employment

At one time, employers, including architects, could hire and fire at will, but the influence of trade unions and others, and various laws, have changed the situation. One of the most important laws governing employment is the Employment Protection (Consolidation) Act of 1978.

The act does not cover self-employed people and certain other groups such as part-time workers. This may be relevant to architects, as some of them employ 'freelance' staff, often supplied by employment agencies. The fact that these self-employed people are not covered by the Employment Protection Act will have financial implications for their employer, and this may even be an inducement to architects, particularly in the early stages of a practice, to make all their staff self-employed.

Most genuine full-time employees will have a Contract of Service. This will be issued within 13 weeks of starting work and will include the names of the parties involved in the contract, the date employment commenced, pay details, hours worked, holiday arrangements, sickness pay, discipline, pension arrangements and notice.

Benefits to the employees include firm rights as to payment of their wages. They pay tax by PAYE, whereas self–employed staff pay tax in half yearly instalments. Employees are Class 1 National Insurance contributors, as opposed to Class 2 for self–employed staff. They also have minimum notice and dismissal rights, are entitled to maternity leave and pay where appropriate, and also enjoy certain rights in respect of trade unions and safety care.

Employees also have legal obligations to their employers in as much as they are expected to render faithful service. This can be relevant for architectural staff who may be tempted to run a small private practice of their own from their employer's office, for they are not legally entitled to make a secret profit from their employer or to compete with them. Also, confidential information is expected to be kept confidential.

A serious breach of contract on either side can result in the ending of the contract without notice. An aggrieved employee can take his case to an Industrial Tribunal.

6.13 Dismissal of employees

Minimum periods of dismissal are fixed by the Employment Protection Act. Employers must give a minimum of one-week notice for each year of service, up to a maximum of

12 weeks. Employees must give a minimum of one-week notice. Periods of notice can be more, or less, by agreement. Employees who consider they have been unfairly dismissed, can apply to an Industrial Tribunal, but they must take action within three months. The possible results of such action may be re-instatement, (i.e. given their old job back); re-engagement (i.e. given a different but comparable job); or compensation.

6.14 Redundancy

Unfortunately the construction industry, including architectural practices, are more susceptible than most to changes in the nation's economic climate. Financial cut-backs frequently lead to a reduction of architectural work, and from time to time, some architects will be faced with the unpleasant task of reducing staff.

Employees with two or more years of continuous employment will, under their Contract of Service, be entitled to redundancy payments.

Valid reasons for redundancy are defined as:

(a) The employer has ceased to carry on his business.

(b) The demand for the employer's business has diminished or ceased.

(c) The employer has moved his office, and the employee is not prepared to move to the new location.

The procedure is that the employer normally pays the redundancy money, but he may be able to obtain 41% from the Redundancy Fund, which is a fund financed by employers and administered by the Department of Employment. If need be the employee can claim direct from the fund. He can also appeal to the Industrial Tribunal.

6.15 National Insurance

All employers have legal obligations regarding deductions for National Insurance. They both deduct the employee's contributions from his salary, and make their own employer's contributions. The system is administered by the State under the Social Security Act of 1975 and benefits include unemployment pay, sickness and industrial injury retirement pensions, and mobility allowances.

Payments are generally linked to income rather than risk. As has already been stated, full-time employees pay Class 1 contributions which entitles them to a fuller range of benefits than self-employed people, who are Class 2 contributors.

6.16 Income tax

Employers have to deduct tax from each employee's wages (unless they are self employed) at rates as specified by the Inland Revenue. The Inland Revenue issues a code number to each individual, which is worked out by a system of allowances, which are deducted from the total earnings to give the taxable pay. Architect employers, like other professions, unfortunately have to pay tax. They are covered by Schedule D of the tax schedules, as opposed to Schedule E for the employees. A full-time working director of a limited liability company is treated as an employee and is therefore covered by Schedule E.

Schedule D covers both sole principals of an architectural practice as well as partnerships. Any profit made has to be declared and the Inland Revenue require to know the net profit for the accounting year, supported by a statement of accounts.

6.17 Holidays

It is not always appreciated that generally, holidays are a matter of agreement between employer and employee, and they are not covered by the Employment Protection Act.

However most employees in Britain get three weeks paid holiday a year and many get more than this. Holiday entitlement will normally be fixed by the Employment Contract, and this is legally binding on both parties.

There will normally be a qualifying period before a new employee is allowed holiday with pay.

7

Design constraints

7.1 Introduction

At the beginning of this book reference was made to the varied skills and breadth of knowledge the architect needs to possess in order to undertake the role of architect effectively.

In developing the design the architect must take account of many constraints, including those imposed by the client's specific and preferred requirements; factors related to sites and their environment; cost considerations; the effects of legal rights and responsibilities; planning and building legislation and procedures, together with controls exercised by the needs of building engineering services and the limitation of constructional techniques. These constraints are discussed in this chapter.

7.2 The client

Clients can be broadly divided into two main groups. Those who build for their own use, and those who build for profit. The first group includes the married couple who want a house to live in; a shopkeeper who needs a shop to trade in; a giant industrial company who wish to have a new industrial complex to manufacture their products; a government department requiring an office block to house their staff, and a church needing a new building in which to worship. The second group includes the contractor who builds houses, shops and factories to sell and let for profit, and insurance companies who build office blocks as a source of investment for their funds.

Both of these two main groups of clients will exercise constraints on the design of the building. There is likely, however, to be more variation in the constraints imposed by the first of these groups – i.e. by the client who will occupy the building he is financing. He will always conceive the idea, but sometimes the concept may be no more than him wanting a house, shop or factory built. This will mean that the architect has to do more work to produce a building matching the client's needs, but he will have the maximum freedom to introduce his own ideas into the design. Another client may have very fixed ideas as to what he wants; sometimes to such an extent that the architect will begin to wonder why he has been employed. In such a case the architect will have to be firm enough to ensure that the client does not exceed his designated role under the terms of the building contract.

The client who builds for speculation will generally have a different attitude to the owner-occupier. His main aim will be to make a profit from the sale of the completed building, so he will generally go to considerable trouble to find out what the public wants, and what they will pay for it. He will then, with the aid of his architect, set himself the task of meeting these requirements, while still making a profit from the enterprise.

Architects must always remember that their role is to act as agents of their clients and to translate their needs, and not always their precise ideas, into the finished building. This is particularly important with the type of client mentioned in the previous paragraph. It is not unknown for such dominant clients to exercise excessive control over the design and construction of a building, and then lay all the blame at the feet of the architect when the completed building does not match up to his expectations.

Another major constraint the client will exercise, will be the amount of money he will have, to finance the project. It must be remembered that the client, either directly or indirectly, pays for everyone involved in the building process, and for all the materials used. The effect of cost limits will be considered later, but for now it is sufficient to state the obvious fact that the amount of money available will influence both the size and quality of the finished building. One of the first questions the architect must therefore ask the client, is how much money he has at his disposal. In some cases the answer might be none, because the client is hoping to fund the entire project with some form of outside financial assistance. In this case the architect will need to proceed with caution, until he is certain that the anticipated financial backing has materialised.

The third constraint the client generally brings with him when he first approaches his architect will be the site. Again this is dealt with in more detail later, but clearly the site the client wants to use for the proposed building, will greatly influence the design.

7.3 User requirements

Buildings are not intended to be monuments to architects, but of use to the people who occupy them. The architect therefore has to ensure that the building is designed to meet the needs of the people who will occupy and use it. This necessitates studies to establish user requirements. There has to be a detailed analysis as to the function of the buildings, and the activities which will take place within it. The required environmental conditions will have to be decided, and requirements on matters as diverse as appearance and toilet requirements agreed.

An example of a factory is used below, to list the sort of questions the architect will need to ask before finalising his studies and design.

(a) What type of process takes place in the factory?

(b) If there are a number of processes, do they have to be separated?

(c) What plant and machinery will be installed?

(d) Are line layouts (illustrating the manufacturing process) and a plant layout (illustrating the layout of plant and equipment) available?

(e) Does the factory have to be single storey, or would a multi-storey building be acceptable?

(f) Does the need for a continuous production line dictate the length of the building?

(g) Is there need for a minimum uninterrupted space across the width which will dictate the bay spacing?

(h) Is there a minimum clear height requirement?

(i) How many people will occupy the factory, and at what hours will they be working? What is the likely proportion of men to women?

(j) What are the requirements for meals, toilet facilities, medical facilities etc?

(k) What level of lighting is required? Is daylighting essential in any areas?

(l) What level of heating is required? Is there a need for air conditioning in any areas?

(m) What will be the noise levels from machines?

(n) Are there any special environmental factors – e.g. fumes, dust?

(o) What loadings are expected from machinery etc?

(p) What degree of security is required?

(q) What services are required to serve the manufacturing process?

(r) Is there a requirement for future expansion?

The above list is by no means exhaustive, but is merely meant to give an indication of the type of questions the architect will have to ask. This will entail a detailed study to establish use requirements and the results will clearly act as a constraint on the design.

7.4 The site

In the initial stages of the design of a building, the architect needs to investigate the site to decide its suitability for the building required by the client. This site investigation is related to the environment, by which we mean the things surrounding the site, including the climate. The site investigation will incorporate the site accesses, boundary features, topography, subsoil, services, and any underground hazards. All of these items are likely to act as constraints in the design of the building.

This is particularly true nowadays when the ideal building site, even if there was ever such a thing, is very hard to find. Difficult sites such as those of awkward shape, or on steeply sloping ground, or having poor subsoil, or uninviting surroundings, will often be developed, whereas in the past they would not be used for building purposes.

Sometimes the architect will be involved in the selection of the site. This is the best arrangement, as a properly trained and experienced architect should be better placed than the lay person to select a site most suitable for the building required by the client.

If there is a choice of sites, it is obviously important to select the best available site the client can afford to buy. This is particularly vital when the building is a speculative venture. The biggest single factor likely to encourage people to buy a new speculative built house is that it is located in an area which the prospective purchasers find attractive. This is obviously linked with the environment, for house owners, and owners of other types of buildings, are clearly concerned with ease of access, local amenities, views, climate, and all the other environmental factors. These will be considered in more detail later.

Even within the boundaries of the site, there will be many factors which will act as constraints on the design of the building.

The first constraint is the actual plan shape of the site. It is rarely possible to build over the whole area of the site. Instead, the available space has to be apportioned between buildings; roads, circulation and parking areas, and landscaped and open spaces. The space allocated to the actual buildings will obviously govern the size and shape of the buildings.

The second factor will be the site contours. A flat site may at first seem advantageous, but it could mean it is susceptible to flooding, particularly if it is low lying. This could affect the decision as to whether or not to include a basement or semi-basement in the building. A steeply sloping site will influence the cost of the building, due to its effect on the type and levels of the foundations. It may also affect the levels of the ground floors, which could affect the design because it results in a split level solution. If the contours are pronounced, it is almost certain to influence the position of the buildings on the site, and it could affect them in other ways, such as the position of the entrances.

The level of the site in relation to the roads outside and the site entrance, will influence the site access and internal road layout.

The orientation of the site, relative to the north point, will also affect the position of accesses, entrances and windows, because the aspect governs the quantity of sun the various elevations receive. There is an obvious advantage in ensuring that the rooms in which people spend most of the daylight hours have the most sun. This may mean for example, that a house on a north facing site may be designed so that the main living rooms are at the back rather than the front of the house.

The subsoil under the site will influence the type of structure, and possibly the height of the building. It is one of the major factors in the cost of the building. If, due to a poor subsoil, the foundation costs are excessive, it will mean that less money is available for other elements of the building. This in turn could affect the overall design of the building. It is advisable – many would say essential – to carry out a soil investigation before proceeding too far with the design, and this is achieved by means of trial holes and boreholes. Information on the type of subsoil, and its safe bearing capacity, is necessary in order to design a safe and an economic building.

The level of the water table – i.e. the level at which water appears naturally in the ground – needs to be established. A high water table may mean a subsoil drainage system needs to be incorporated into the design if flooding is to be avoided. It will also affect the floor levels, as there is a strong case for keeping all floors above the expected water table level.

Consideration should be given to any existing physical features on the site which could enhance the setting of the proposed building. There could be a lake, or some attractive mature trees which need to be retained. This could mean siting the building outside these physical features, or even incorporating them within an internal courtyard around which the building is designed. Either way the siting and design of the building is likely to be affected. There may also be some existing buildings on the site which need to be retained, or incorporated within the new buildings. If so, these will also act as a constraint on the design.

Again, existing services, either below or above ground level, can influence the location of the building on the site, and could in some cases restrict the size of the building. They could also affect the position of those rooms requiring service connections. Service items are discussed in more detail later under Section 7.10.

The factors mentioned above will all be included in the site investigation undertaken as part of Stage B (feasibility) of the RIBA Plan of Work. This is discussed in Section 10.3 of Chapter 10.

7.5 Environment

As has already been stated, the environment, by which is meant the things surrounding the site, is often of particular importance to the prospective occupier of a building, and is likely to influence and act as a constraint on the design of the building.

The occupier will probably not only prefer a site which is itself pleasantly contoured and landscaped, but also one which has pleasant views surrounding it. If a particular side of the site looks out on to attractive countryside, this is likely to affect the siting of the building and the location of windows. Similarly, if another side of the site has a less attractive outlook, such as a railway line or motorway, the designer is likely to position the less important rooms on that side of the building. If existing buildings surround certain parts of the site, the architect may plan his building to avoid looking out onto the existing structures, in order to ensure the maximum privacy for the building's occupiers. It can be appreciated therefore that the existing landscape and buildings surrounding the site are likely to influence the juxtaposition of the building and the position of the windows.

The occupier of any type of building is likely to need access to various facilities, including transport services, and this will influence the position of the site and building entrances.

Climate is another factor which acts as a constraint on building design, and affects the siting and appearance of buildings. In the tropics for example, where the sun is too hot and too bright, the aim is more likely to be in keeping the sunlight out of the building, rather than letting it in. In the dry tropics this has resulted in the traditional house having thick walls and small windows, whilst in the humid tropics the buildings are likely to incorporate devices such as canopies, overhangs, and louvres, so as to shade the walls without restricting the flow of air.

Traditionally in the UK, windows are likely to be of various shapes and sizes, depending on the use of the room, their aspect, and views. The architect has to decide on the purpose of the windows – e.g. lighting, ventilation, views – before he can decide the best shapes and sizes.

The aspect of the site is obviously of considerable importance, because it will govern the total number of hours of sunshine a building will receive, and at what time of the day. There is no legal requirement which states that a habitable room must have sunlight, although there is a Code of Practice which recommends that every living room should have at least one hour of sunshine a day, during at least ten months a year.

There is also a recommended daylight factor for various types of buildings, which is represented as a percentage of the illumination for a point indoors as compared to a point outdoors. For example an entrance hall needs one percent, and a bank needs two percent. This need for daylight will influence the shape of the rooms and building. Various charts and other aids are available to give the conditions for different rooms and skies, but as a generalisation a rectangular room with windows in the long wall will be better lit than if the same area of windows are in one of the short walls.

Whilst the aspect will be the main factor governing the amount of sunlight entering a building, other factors, such as the slope of the ground, and the shape, size and position of surrounding buildings, will also have a part to play.

There will be some situations, even in the UK, where sunlight needs to be controlled. Examples are art galleries, museums and libraries containing valuable books where direct sunlight could damage the contents, and also exits from garage areas where sun dazzle could adversely affect the car drivers.

The architect also needs to consider the expected rainfall on a building, both to design the drainage system correctly, and to make the correct decisions which would prevent rain penetration. The use of flat roofs need to be considered with care, as there have been cases in recent years where they have resulted in rain penetration. Invariably this has been due to incorrect design and construction, but there is a case for saying that the problem can often be more easily solved by using a fairly steeply sloping roof. Obviously such a decision will affect the appearance of the building.

Sometimes, however, a flat roof will be a logical choice. In the Middle East for example, where there is a low rainfall, and due to the hot weather the inhabitants may wish to sleep on the roof, the roof is more likely to be flat. Admittedly, the rain, when it comes, may fall in quite large amounts, but the people of these areas often have a more enlightened attitude to roof maintenance than inhabitants of the UK, so flat roofs tend to create fewer problems.

The problem of rain penetration is linked with wind pressure, as wind can often drive rain into buildings, particularly through places such as window openings. The prevailing winds in the UK, are from the West. The direction of the wind will affect decisions, such as the location of walkways and entrances. The architect will also take account of other factors such as the fact that conditions tend to be uncomfortable for pedestrians when the wind is blowing and they are walking in a gap between high and low buildings.

Wind effect will also be affected by the surrounding landscape. Trees will often provide shelter and affect the wind flow. Again the shape of buildings will affect their strength in certain directions, and their ability to resist wind pressure. If the expected wind force on a wall is considerable, it will have to be strong enough to resist such pressures, and this will influence the construction and materials used. The lifting of lightweight roofs by suction also needs to be considered in areas of high wind pressure, with particular care taken with regard to problems from roof overhangs.

Snow is less likely to be a problem in the UK, but the designer will need to consider the weight of snow on the roof. He will bear in mind the possibility of snow finding its way into the building if there is a defect in the roof, and consider whether this is more likely to happen with a flat roof rather than a pitched one.

It will be readily appreciated that climate varies considerably from country to country, but it is also true that there are variations between various parts of the United Kingdom. Records kept by the Meteorological Office indicate that, generally the northern and eastern parts of the country are colder than the South, and the West is the wettest part of the country. Designers and contractors often make use of the weather man to help them create buildings which will mitigate the worst effects of our climate.

The amount of dust, salt, sand, and man made additions to the air, such as wastes from chimneys, will affect the degree of pollution surrounding the building. The resulting pollution may damage people's health, and also adversely affect building materials. This will inevitably influence the choice of building materials, and hence the appearance of the building.

Noise, originating from places such as airfields, railways, motor traffic routes, industry, and public playgrounds, is another factor the architect should consider. This will affect the siting of the building, as regards to keeping it as far away as possible from noise sources. Particular care will be taken with the location of rooms requiring quiet conditions, including the positioning and sizes of windows and other openings.

7.6 Cost limits

Cost limits are an important constraint on the design of a building, because the amount of money the client is able and willing to spend will control its size and quality. It is often said that you get what you pay for, and this is certainly true of buildings. There are very few cases when an architect is told by the client to proceed with the design regardless of costs. Generally there is a limit to what the client can afford, so the architect, with the aid of the quantity surveyor, has the responsibility of ensuring that design and construction of the building is subjected to cost limits, cost planning and cost control.

Cost limits dictate the total amount of money the client is able to spend on a project. The design team ensures that the cost limit figure is not exceeded by means of cost planning and cost control.

Cost planning means allocating the available money between the different parts of the building, generally in respect of elements such as substructure, floors, roof, walls, doors/windows, stairs, finishes, services etc. As the amount of money the client has to spend is generally limited, it means that in practice, if a disproportionate sum is spent on one item, there will be less money available for the other items. A factory owner may be less concerned about the appearance of his building that the annual running costs. He may therefore want the architect to economise on the cladding so that more money is available for insulation and an efficient heating system. Again, a speculative builder may decide to spend money on luxury kitchens and bathrooms in his houses, because he believes this will make them easier to sell. However, this may lead him to save money on items the purchasers are less likely to notice, such as the roof construction and drainage.

It can be seen therefore that cost planning is part of the design process, because decisions on the allocation of money have to be made at the design stage, and will clearly influence the appearance of the building. These decisions may also affect the size of the building, because there will often be a choice between a smaller building with high standards of construction and finishes, or a larger building constructed to minimal standards.

Cost control starts at the design stage, and continues throughout the job. It means checking costs at all stages, to ensure that the client's cost limits are not exceeded. If more money is spent on one element than was planned, money will have to be saved elsewhere to avoid exceeding the cost limits.

The duration of the project, in respect of both design and construction time, also has an effect on costs, and could act as a constraint on the design of the building. This is due to the fact that costs are continually escalating, because of inflation and increases in the cost of labour and materials during the life of the project. The architect may make a decision to simplify the design and construction of the building as much as possible so as to reduce the programme time, and minimise the effect of inflation. This will affect the appearance of the building.

The architect, as part of the design process, also needs to consider the cost of maintenance. Maintenance costs are often related to correct design, and to decisions as to whether it is worthwhile paying for better, more robust materials, and the best available workmanship, so as to reduce future maintenance costs.

The subject of maintenance is connected with cost in use of a building. This consists of:

(a) Annual equivalent worth of initial expenditure on the building plus

(b) Average recurring costs – i.e. items such as maintenance, replacement, decorations, running costs of services etc.

It may be that over a period of, say 60 years, a poor quality building which only just meets the requirements of the building and other regulations, costs more as an average every year than a good quality building. This is because in the poor quality building there are extra costs for maintenance, replacements, decorations and running costs, which do not occur on a good quality building with the best workmanship and materials; self-finished surfaces; high insulation and an efficient heating system.

In working out the cost for a 60-year period, the accumulated costs (total of initial expenditure plus recurring costs for 60 years) must be divided by 60 to give the annual cost. Allowance must be made for interest on money not used for initial expenditure, and for the cost of borrowing extra money to finance a more expensive building initially.

When the architect presents the proposed design to the client, it will need to be accompanied by an estimate of the cost. Clients will often view the cost aspect with regard to the following.

(a) The total cost of the project.

(b) The cost value.

(c) The effect of the building market on the cost.

In looking at the total cost of the project, the client will need to satisfy himself, that an equivalent building could not be obtained at less cost from some other source. It is possible for example, that a person wanting a bungalow built on her site may discover a timber system built bungalow, which would meet all her needs, is available at a much cheaper price than the traditional design offered by her architect.

Again, an industrialist may be disappointed by the high cost of an architect's design, and turn to a design and build contractor to provide a new factory.

The client will also consider the cost value; or how valuable the completed building will be to him. Above all he will want to assure himself that the building is economically viable. There is clearly little value for example, in an industrialist having a factory built; equipping it, starting production, and then discovering that his profit is less than he would have obtained from putting his money in a deposit account at the bank.

The third fact to consider will be the economic factors at the time building operations are about to begin. It could happen that, due to a lot of people wanting work undertaken at a particular time, and a shortage of labour and materials, that building costs are escalating. If, as would probably be the case, a fluctuation clause is included in the contract, the client may decide that these additional costs mean that the project is no longer viable. In such circumstances the client may either cancel the project, or else wait until the building market is more favourable to clients.

All the above factors will act as a considerable restraint on the design.

7.7 Legal requirements

The law is concerned with rules which society agrees to obey, in order to follow an acceptable way of life. There are two main groups of laws. Common law is unwritten, and follows custom and precedent, relying on the binding decisions of judges. Legislative law is law made or approved by Parliament, and includes orders in Council, statutory instruments, and bye-laws. Sanctions are imposed as an aid to enforcing the law, and these may take the form of fines, imprisonment, or the awarding of damages.

The law affecting construction work is complicated and extensive, and acts as a considerable constraint on the design of the building. It includes the law of property and land, environmental powers, including statutory consents and planning law, copyright law, and laws relating to building contracts.

Whilst the architect is not expected to have the legal knowledge of a lawyer, he is expected to have a working knowledge of the law for all matters, which in any way affects his role as the client's agent. In addition he will be expected to have a detailed knowledge of those matters, such as the building regulations and building contracts, which are his direct concern.

The law of property and land may influence the design of a building in respect of matters such as boundaries, easements, restrictive covenants, and landlord and tenant covenants.

Boundaries may be marked by fences, hedges, ditches, walls, roads, rivers or streams. The architect needs to establish the exact position of the boundaries, not only to ensure that all building work is carried out on land which the client actually owns, but also because exact distances from building faces to boundary lines are relevant to conformity with certain building regulations.

An easement is a right benefitting the owner of one piece of land over the owner of another piece of land. These easements are transferred with the land if it is sold. Examples are the right to pass over someone's land; or to lay drains under someone else's land. If easements such as these are granted, they may affect the siting of the building, because of the need to avoid the position of the right of way or the drain route.

The architect will also need to remember that adjoining land owners may have a right of support from his client's land. In designing the building, the architect must ensure it will not involve excavations, which will mean the withdrawal of support to the adjacent land.

The adjoining owner may also have acquired a right to light, and this could influence the siting and height of the building. Daylighting requirements are also affected by building and planning regulations.

Restrictive covenants are restrictions on the use of one piece of land to the benefit of the owners of other land. Such covenants may dramatically affect the design of a building. An example is that of a man who sells off part of his garden as building land. In order to protect the enjoyment of his own house, he may include a restrictive covenant in the conveyance that only a bungalow may be built on the land, and the appearance must be in character with the surrounding properties.

Landlord and tenant covenants may affect the architect undertaking work in buildings which the client leases, rather than owns. The architect must make sure that he does not remove or alter parts which are regarded as landlord's fixtures.

Planning laws affect all developments with a few minor exceptions, such as small additions to buildings. Permission has to be obtained from the planning authority before work can take place. Planning laws are particularly concerned with the appearance of buildings, their size and siting, and ensuring they will be in character with the surrounding areas. Generally, planning laws are the most important single restraint on the design of a building. They are discussed in Section 7.9 of this chapter.

Building regulations are concerned with the construction of buildings, rather than their appearance. They are intended to ensure that the design and construction of a building will be such as to ensure public health and safety. These also act as a considerable constraint on the designer, and their effect is discussed in more detail in Section 7.8 of this chapter.

There are many other acts which the architect has to take account of in designing a building. Examples are the Health and Safety at Work Act of 1974; Factory Acts of 1961; Offices, Shops and Railway Premises Acts of 1963 and Fire Precautions Act of 1971.

There is an incredible range of legislation which can be loosely linked together under the heading of environmental laws. These include laws which affect the architect and constrain his design, such as compulsory purchase, housing, pollution and highways acts. There is only space here to mention a few examples.

Architects will sometimes be involved in design and construction work to existing houses, and in such circumstances they must take account of the various housing acts. This means ensuring the completed house is fit for human habitation; repairing drains and w.cs properly; allowing for the removal of refuse; providing bathrooms or shower rooms; and in the case of multiple occupied housing, arranging suitable means of escape in case of fire.

The architect should also be aware as to the position regarding improvement grants, so that the client may benefit financially as much as possible from the available grants.

There are a range of pollution laws which are intended to prevent people's health being endangered. They include clean air acts to avoid air pollution; public health acts to prevent water pollution; noise abatement acts to minimise noise nuisances, and other acts affecting the storage of refuse. All of these acts, to a lesser or greater degree, can have ramifications on the design of a building.

The various highways acts can also affect the architect's design. An example is the 1980 Highways Act, under which the highway authority can prescribe an improvement line – that is to say a proposed widening of a street. This means land will be taken off the adjacent sites, and should therefore be taken into account by the architect when he sites his proposed building. Another example is the Highways Act 1959 which allows the local authority to require all buildings erected at the junction of two streets to have rounded or splayed corners. The 1971 Act allows a highway authority to prevent private accesses to a public highway.

The architect also needs to take account of the law of copyright. One would normally expect the architect to produce an original design for a building. There may be occasions however when the project consists of extending an existing building by another architect. In such a case the client might insist that the extension should copy the style of the original building. Again, the client may give his architect a sketch of a building designed by another architect, and ask that certain features shown on the sketch be incorporated in his proposed building. In such cases, the architect must make sure he does not infringe another architect's copyright. This has a constraining effect on the architect's design.

7.8 Building regulations

Most building work in England and Wales operates under the Building Regulations of 1985. (NB Scotland has its own regulations). As has been previously stated, the main purpose of the regulations is to ensure that buildings are properly constructed so as to ensure the health and safety of people in and about buildings. The regulations, together with their supporting documents, are comprehensive and exercise a considerable constraint on the design and construction of buildings.

The regulations are set out in 11 parts – Parts A to L (excluding I) – plus a separate schedule detailing facilities for disabled people. They are supported by 11 advisory approved documents, and 1 mandatory document, which give practical guidance on ways of meeting the regulations. Some of the approved documents refer to British Standards or Agre'ment Certificates. If you choose not to follow the guidance given in the approved documents, you can devise your own solutions to meet the requirements of the regulations.

Listed below are the various parts of the regulations, with examples as to how they might exercise a constraint on the design and construction of a building.

Part A: Structure will affect the size and spacing of columns and beams; the thickness of walls; and the number, size and position of openings.

Part B: Fire will affect the arrangement of corridors and staircases, and the construction of elements of structure, including the size and position of wall openings.

Part C: Site preparation and resistance to moisture will affect the construction, and hence the appearance, of floors, walls and roofs.

Part D: Toxic substances will affect the types of insulating material used in the cavities of cavity walls, with a marginal effect on the cost and construction.

Part E: Sound will affect the construction, and hence the appearance of walls and floors, due to the need of resistance to the passage of sound.

Part F: Ventilation will marginally affect the appearance, due to the necessary measures needed to provide room ventilation.

Part G: Hygiene will marginally affect the planning and appearance of parts of the building, due to the necessary acceptable standard of hygiene in respect of food storage, bathrooms, hot water and sanitary convenience.

Part H: Drainage waste disposal will marginally affect the planning of the building, due to the necessary provision of a satisfactory drainage system.

Part J: Heat producing appliances will affect the appearance of the building in the vicinity of fireplaces, stoves, etc., due to the necessary requirements in designing and constructing these areas, so that they will not constitute a fire hazard.

Part K: Staircases and ramps will affect the appearance of staircases and ramps, as they have to be constructed so as to ensure that people using them are afforded a safe passage.

Part L: Conservation of fuel and power will affect the appearance of buildings due to the necessary choice of materials, and limited window areas, so as to achieve prescribed standards of thermal insulation.

Schedule 2: Facilities for disabled people will marginally affect the planning and appearance of buildings, due to the necessary provision of acceptable standards of access, and where appropriate, wheelchair spaces for disabled people.

Information regarding the extent of building work is controlled by the building regulations, together with details of the system of building control, is given in Section 8.20 of Chapter 8.

7.9 Town planning acts

The Town and Country Planning Acts give local authorities a wide range of powers to control development in their area. Development plans are prepared by the County and District Councils, with dual aims of protecting the natural and built environments, and achieving a balanced allocation of the available land to meet various needs – i.e. housing, industrial, recreational etc. In exercising this control, the local authorities apply a considerable constraint on the design and appearance of buildings.

The first constraint is to control the class of building allowed in a particular area – i.e. domestic, office, factory etc. This is achieved by Structure Plans prepared by County Councils and Local Plans produced by District (Borough) Councils, which zone different areas for different purposes, including Green Belt land.

Development control introduces an additional constraint to that of zoning. It controls the density of the proposed development – e.g. in the case of a housing development it might stipulate a maximum number of dwellings per hectare. It could limit the size of a building on a particular plot, or the height, either in metres or the number of storeys.

The actual appearance of the building will also often be controlled. This is almost certain to be the case with areas designated as Conservation Areas, which are considered to include natural and built environment of special interest. Developments in such places will have to be in accord with the special visual quality of the area. However, even in other areas, the appearance of proposed buildings will generally expect to be in sympathy with that of the existing buildings.

Information regarding the extent of buildings work controlled by the Planning Acts, together with details of the planning application system, is given in Section 8.21 of Chapter 8.

7.10 Building services

Building services are generally assumed to include hot and cold water supplies, above and below ground drainage, including sanitary appliances, refuse disposal, heating, ventilation, air conditioning, electrical installations including lighting, telecommunications, gas installations, fire protection, mechanical conveyors and security systems.

The total cost of these services, including plant, ducts, pipes and cables, together with the space allocated in the building to accommodate the services is a major cost factor in most buildings. The percentage figure may vary between 20–60% of the total cost of the building.

Building services are used as a device to vary the environment within a building, and create acceptable conditions inside when conditions outside are totally unacceptable. In practice people can only exist within a limited range of temperatures, without taking special steps to mitigate the effects of the climate.

The extent to which building services will influence the overall design of the building will depend on the use and complexity of the building.

In some buildings special environmental conditions need to be created, and this will influence the whole form of the building. An example is a factory manufacturing items such as computer tapes which need to be produced under clean room conditions. In such a building, the conditioned air needs to be absolutely clean, so the plant rooms might be placed on the roof of the clean room, and the air would flow from holes in a filtered ceiling downwards through the room into a perforated floor, and then back up to the high level plant room via vertical ducts at the sides of the room.

In another building the manufacturing process might involve extensive services, and controlled light and heating conditions. The client might require a windowless box with artificial lighting and a sophisticated heating system involving a high standard of insulation. The form and appearance of such a factory will be largely influenced by the building services needs. Even in buildings, where the services are less complicated and restrictive, there will be about 10% of the floor area allocated to plant items and vertical ducts. There will also be the need for floor ducts, and voids in the ceiling spaces to houses services. The location of these items will have an influence on the overall design.

Consideration of building services are less critical in conventional houses, but space still has to be allocated, generally in the roof, for water tanks, pipes and cables, and there will be a need to provide at least some wall chases and accommodation for cables and small pipes.

It is important to consider building services at the initial design stage. Space for major plant items such as boilers, air conditioning equipment, and sub-station equipment has to be selected and allocated to suit the most efficient operation of the building services.

Apart from occupying space and influencing the overall layout, plant provision tends to affect the elevations, as plant rooms generally need to be provided with louvres, grilles, and special accesses, and may be of different heights to other parts of the building. Sometimes the plant rooms may be located on the roof, or even in separate buildings. The decision as to the exact routes of the ducts for the services distribution system will clearly have an effect on the overall planning. The type of heat emitters, grilles and other terminal devices will affect the inside appearance of the building. Consideration of heating and air conditioning is linked with insulation, and the size and position of windows, as well as orientation. It can be seen therefore that the building services will affect the overall cost, shape, size, appearance and orientation of the building.

It will also have a considerable effect on the construction programme. As the services content of most buildings is relatively high, it will have to be carefully integrated into the overall programme, so that it can be completed as quickly as possible, and achieve continuity of work. The incorporation of builder's ducts within the design to accommodate the distribution of all services will assist in this aim. It will also be helpful in effectively maintaining the completed building.

The ducts provide a space through which services pass; either conditioned air fed directly into the duct, or services such as gas, water and drainage pipes, and electrical cables.

Ducts have many functions. The most obvious one is to conceal the services, thus improving the appearance of the building. They also prevent services becoming a nuisance to the occupiers of the building, due to noise from pipes or ducts, danger from hot pipes, and dust catching ledges. The ducts themselves also give protection from physical and other damage. Further advantages are to allow easy installation, independent of the remaining construction operations; easy inspection, maintenance, and replacement; facilitation of alterations and additions. It also tends to discipline the service designers and installers as to where they locate the pipes and cables etc.

The following are the main types of ducts which the architect needs to incorporate into his design:

(a) Main horizontal ducts, which are commonly at ground level, but may be at roof level, particularly in respect of air ducts.

(b) Main vertical ducts which link services to each floor.

(c) Lateral subsidiary ducts which provide local horizontal distribution and may be in ceiling voids.

In terms of size, there are walk ducts with a minimum height of 2 metres; crawl ducts with a minimum height of 1 metre; and recessed ducts and casings which have space for the services, but no working space inside the duct.

The ducts may be prefabricated and supplied by the services sub-contractor, but generally some, if not all of them, will be constructed by the main contractor in materials such as brickwork, blockwork and reinforced concrete.

The availability and location of the public services can also act as a constraint on the design. If services are not available it will mean for example that electricity will have to be privately generated, and sewage treated within the site, which clearly has cost and other implications.

There could be restrictions on the use of public services. An industrialist, for example, might need to use large quantities of water for his manufacturing process and the authority responsible for the sewers might not permit this volume of water to discharge into the system during the daytime, as it would overload the sewers. This could mean storing the waste water in large tanks, so that it can be discharged into the public sewers in the evenings when the volume of water in the sewers is much less.

Public service authorities may have other special requirements as a condition of supplying their service. For example, electricity boards commonly require large users of electricity (such as industrialists) to provide transformer chambers within their premises.

Even in public services are available when required, their actual position may influence the siting of the building, if an economical arrangement of building services is to be achieved.

7.11 The contractor

During the design process the architect should spare a thought for the contractor. In the interests of everyone, including the client, the architect should design his/her building in such a way that the contractor's job is made as easy as possible. Whilst it is accepted that virtually anything is possible, if an architect has a reputation for unusually complicated detailing which makes his buildings difficult to construct, the contractor is likely to take account of this fact when preparing his tender, and the client will pay extra for his architect's bad reputation.

This does not mean that the architect must necessarily abandon aesthetics for the practicalities of building, but he should keep the method of construction as simple as possible. As a general rule, if something is easy to draw, it is likely to be easy to build.

Sometimes it will be possible to design so as to suit a rationalised system of construction. This means, for example, ensuring as far as possible, that items of construction are not interdependent on each other; using integrated components where feasible, and having the minimum number of different components.

Care should be taken to design elements which are easy to fix, and which suit the contractor's plant – e.g. to relate the size and weight of units to the cranage likely to be available. It is helpful if the structure can be designed in a way that facilitates stability during the construction process. Concrete work is often an expensive and time-consuming part of the construction and for *in situ* work the formwork is the major element. The architect can assist in this area by producing a design where the formwork is as uncomplicated as possible, with simple profiles, bold splays, and no square arrises. It should also be recognised that construction joints are difficult to hide, and that large uninterrupted areas of exposed smooth concrete are best avoided. Where acceptable, dry techniques, particularly in respect of finishes, can help the contractor achieve a fast programme.

As regards to services, it is an advantage if these can be installed independently of the structure and finishes, as far as possible – e.g. by the maximum use of ducts, which are designed with the building, and not added as an afterthought.

It is obviously also vital that the architect prepares his production information in a manner and order to suit the contractor's programme. It is not suggested that the architect should know as much about the practicalities of building as the experienced contractor, or do anything likely to prejudice the quality of his design or the client's interest. He should however be sympathetic and knowledgeable about the contractor's problems, and where possible specify methods which will assist the contractor to do his work quickly and efficiently.

Design procedures generally

8.1 Introduction

There are some aspects of the procedures that the designer follows, which are of interest and relevance at all stages of a project. They include the RIBA Plan of Work, production information, the contract, and various statutory regulations. These matters are discussed in this chapter.

8.2 RIBA plan of Work

In order to fulfil his role effectively as a client's agent, the architect has to organise his business in a logical way. It is easier to do this if he adopts a series of routine procedures for every contract. The RIBA publishes a Job Book which outlines the way in which the architect should administer a building project both at the pre-contract and contract stages. The Architect's Job Book details the various stages of the RIBA Plan of Work. Although it is comprehensive and describes all the activities the architect needs to undertake, it is flexible enough to suit the requirements of any project.

The various stages are as follows:

Stage A:	Inception.
Stage B:	Feasibility.
Stage C:	Outline proposals.
Stage D:	Scheme design.
Stage E:	Detail design.
Stage F:	Production information.
Stage G:	Bills of quantities.
Stage H:	Tender action.
Stage J:	Project planning.
Stage K:	Operations on site.
Stage L:	Completion.
Stage M:	Feedback.

There are some items of work which will be repeated at most stages. These are as follows:

(a) Prepare office resources for each stage of the job.

(b) Keep records and files up to date.

(c) Keep client 'in the picture', particularly in respect of matters affecting programme or costs.

(d) Circulate relevant information to all members of the design team.

(e) Confirm everything in writing, using an agreed form of communication.

(f) Check that the project is proceeding in accordance with agreed programme and cost limits.

(g) Check that design office costs and staff resources are not being exceeded.

(h) Make sure that nothing is done contrary to statutory requirements.

(i) Ensure all fees and other charges are paid as they become due.

(j) On completion of one stage prepare for the next stage.

8.3 Contracts

A contract is a legally binding agreement. Contracts are commonly made in writing, although in most cases this is not essential. There are however certain conditions which must apply including the following.

(a) A contract is only valid when an offer has been accepted. In other words both parties must have accepted an agreement.

(b) Both parties must be able to enter legally into a contract – e.g. they must be at least 18 years and of sound mind.

(c) The contract must be legal and possible.

(d) Both parties must derive benefit from the contract – e.g. one party may have a building built for him and the other party may receive money for undertaking the work.

Building contracts are mainly between the client, known as the employer, and the builder, known as the contractor. Each of these parties may be a single person or a group of persons, although if it is a group of persons such as a company, someone clearly has to sign the contract on behalf of the company.

In the construction industry it is common practice to use standard forms of contract prepared by a body known as the Joint Contracts Tribunal (JCT). The JCT forms of contract are prepared by representatives of various bodies, such as the RIBA, RICS, BEC (formerly NFBTE) and local authorities. The main sub-divisions are by the type of employer and the form of pricing. This results in the following JCT forms of contract:

> Standard form, Local authorities, with quantities.
> Standard form, Local authorities, without quantities.
> Standard form, Local authorities, with approximate quantities.
> Standard form, private, with quantities.

Standard form, private, without quantities.
Standard form, private, with approximate quantities.

There is also a form of agreement for minor building works (Minor Works Form) which is a very abbreviated form of the standard edition.

A more recent addition to the JCT standard forms of contract is the JCT Intermediate Form of Building Contract (1984). This was devised because there was felt to be a need for a contract which was less complicated than JCT 80 Standard forms, but not as simplified as the Minor Works Form 1980. The Intermediate Form of Building Contract (IFC84) is produced in a single edition for use by both private individuals and companies, and local authorities.

A Prime Cost Form of Contract is also available for use where prior estimating is impractical, and the contractor is paid for the costs incurred by him (prime costs) plus a fixed fee. Government departments use their own forms of contract for major works and small works.

There are also special Scottish forms of contract, which are necessary because the Scottish legal system is different to the English system. Other forms of standard contract include a sub-contract form for use between the main contractor and sub-contractor, as well as different forms for civil engineering contracts.

The type of standard contract used will depend on the type of job. Clearly the JCT private edition contract will be used for private employers, whether a single individual or a large company. The JCT local authority contract will be used for local authority work.

The differences between the private edition and the local authority edition are relatively small. For example the term architect is used in the private edition, and the term supervising officer in the local authority edition. Other examples are that the local authority edition has provision regarding avoidance of corruption and payment of fair wages.

The edition with quantities are used for most large jobs; the edition without quantities for small jobs, such as a single house; and the edition with approximate quantities for jobs where the bills of quantities are not precise and there needs to be special provision for measurement at the end of the contract.

The Minor Works Form is used for very small jobs, like a house extension, or maintenance contracts where no specialist work is involved.

The Intermediate Form of Building Contract is used where the work is straightforward and does not involve any complex specialist work. Typically it will be used for contracts of a value up to £250,000, but may also be suitable for contracts of a greater value.

Prime cost contracts are generally used in conditions of uncertainty, but where once the contact has been signed there will not be alterations to the nature or scope of the works.

From the contracts mentioned above – which is not an exhaustive list – it can be seen that there are a considerable number of standard forms of contract. Such forms are prepared and used because they are considered to have the following advantages.

(a) It saves time to use a contract which is immediately available, rather than having to prepare a new contract for each project.

(b) It is detailed and fair to all parties as it is the result of much time, effort and expertise.

(c) People become familiar with the document by constant use.

The Standard JCT Forms of Contract (1980) consist of the following parts.

Articles of agreement
This is where the parties sign the contract, and the architect and quantity surveyor are named.

Part 1: general conditions
This part contains 34 clauses, including contractor's obligations, architect's instructions, variations, extension of time, and certificates and payments. Some of the items are dealt with elsewhere in this book, but for more detailed coverage, the reader is advised to refer to the excellent books on the subject of building contracts including those listed in the bibliography of this book.

Part 2: nominated sub-contractors and nominated suppliers
This consists of two clauses, one of which deals with sub-contractors and the other with suppliers.

Part 3: fluctuations
This part deals with ways in which fluctuations in the price of labour and materials will be dealt with.

Appendix
This part, together with the Articles of agreement, gives the contract its individuality. It states the contract particulars, including the start and finishing dates.

In addition to the contract itself, the contract documents consist of the contract drawings and a priced copy of the bill of quantities. If the form of contract is a 'without quantities' edition, a specification will be used instead.

When the contract has been signed, the contractor is entitled to a certified copy of the bills of quantities, a contract, a further unpriced copy of the bills, and two copies of the contract drawings. One copy of the drawings and unpriced bills should be kept on the site.

8.4 Production information

Production information is the total information the design team produces, in order to facilitate the erection of the building. In the wildest sense it will consist of more than just drawings. There are generally, in all but the smallest jobs, four ways in which the contractor and others receive information – drawings, schedules, specifications and bills of quantities.

8.5 Importance of accuracy

It is vital that production information is absolutely clear and easy to understand. Care must be taken to avoid errors, and conflicting inadequate and incomplete information, as this, at best, will lead to indecision and delays at site and elsewhere, and at worst to mistakes in the finished building. The use of drawing check lists can help achieve a comprehensive set of drawings. (See Section 13.4 of Chapter 13).

8.6 Drawings

This is the main medium the designer uses to convey his requirements to everyone else involved in the building project.

The architect and technician will need to remember that, to some extent, each person requires different information. The building control officer for example is mainly concerned that the drawings comply with the building regulations. Structural engineers are mainly concerned with the architect's intentions regarding overall dimensions, beam and column sizes and spacings, use of buildings, loadings and exposure. The building services engineer is mainly concerned with duct spaces, acceptable positions of holes in the structure, fixing positions, and allocation of plant areas. The contractor of course needs detailed information about everything, as he is involved in obtaining materials and components, and employing labour and plant in order to erect the building.

8.7 Drawing structures

The designer has the choice of structuring his drawings in the following ways.

Types of information
The drawings are divided into the following types:

(a) *Location drawings*: They show where the work will be, but may not show how the work is to be performed.

(b) *Assembly drawings*: They show how the building is put together on site.

(c) *Component drawings*: They show details of items manufactured on and off-site.

Further details of 'types of information' drawing structures are given in Section 8.8.

Trade arrangement
This system owes its origin to the days when there were no main contractors and each trade had a separate contract and set of drawings. Nowadays each trade is not so clearly defined, and projects are often more complicated, so the system is less frequently employed.

Operational arrangement
This method was devised by the BRE, based on operational bills. The drawings are arranged to illustrate site operations performed by a man or gang between definite breaks in activities. For example the brickwork from d.p.c to first floor level.

Hybrid system
In this system drawings relate to specific parts of the building – e.g. elements such as the building frame.

8.8 Types of information structure

The commonest drawing structure is 'type of information', so further details of this system are given below.

Location drawings
Location drawings give an overall impression of the building and provide key dimensions to set out the whole building; locate spaces and parts such as doors and windows; and give a key as to where more detailed information can be obtained. Location drawings include:

(a) *Site plans*: These locate the buildings, roads, landscaping etc. on the site and generally provide information regarding levels. They are commonly drawn to a scale of 1:200 and 1:500.
(b) *Floor plans*: These locate spaces such as rooms, and parts such as doors and windows. The most useful scale is probably 1:100, but 1:200 and 1:50 are also used, and occasionally 1:20 or 1:25.
(c) *Sections*: These give a vertical view of the building, including information on overall vertical dimensions and levels. They are drawn to the same scales as the floor plans.
(d) *Elevations*: These show the external faces of the buildings. They are drawn to the same scale as the floor plans.

Assembly drawings
Assembly drawings provide detailed information as to the construction of the building. They commonly consist of sectional plans and vertical sections. Examples are details of window openings, details of the junction between a floor and wall, and between a column and a wall. Common scales are 1:5, 1:10 and 1:20.

Component drawings
Component drawings give full information about components such as doors and windows. Elevations are generally drawn to a scale of 1:100, 1:50 or 1:20, and sections to a scale of 1:20, 1:10 or 1:5.

8.9 Computer Aided Design and draughting (CAD)

In recent years increasing use has been made of computerised design and draughting systems, and prices have now reached a level where even the smaller architectural practices can afford a sophisticated micro system.

The use made of computers will vary from office to office. The term computer aided design is widely used, but a computer system which can design as well as draw and has capacity to produce both 2D and 3D graphical solutions from tabulated data is likely to be expensive and may be out of the reach of smaller firms. It is more usual for computers to be used as automated draughting systems. The design stage of a project is often carried out in a traditional way, and even when a perspective drawing is produced with the aid of a computer it may be finished off manually. Frequently the computer only comes into its own at the working (production) drawing stage.

Initially there may not seem to be a big advantage in using a CAD system for the preparation of working drawings. For example, the saving in time by using a CAD system for producing a location floor plan as opposed to drawing it manually may not be very dramatic. The real advantage comes when drawings have to be ammended, or partly or wholly reproduced for use as structural and services drawings etc., as these operations can be done easily and quickly with CAD.

A typical computer aided draughting system will consist of an alphanumeric keyboard, a graphics display unit, a disc drive, a plotter or line printer, and a menu digester or hand cursor.

The keyboard is similar to a typewriter keyboard with a combination of letters, figures and symbols. The graphics display unit, or visual display unit (VDU) is similar to a television screen, and is where the computer operator sees the drawing being built up.

Some systems use a digitiser board with an input for feeding instructions into the computer made by using a light pen. Others use a hand held cursor, sometimes called a 'mouse' on account of its shape.

Printers provide copies in paper form of the drawing the computer produces, and are generally used where A4 sized drawings are acceptable. Printers producing larger drawings are available but are considerably more expensive, and at the moment are not widely used.

When larger scale drawings are required these will generally be produced by means of a plotter. These are in effect an automatic drawing board, and are available in A3, A2, A1 and A0 sizes. They are also available with single pens, or multi-pens. The multi-pens are more expensive, but they enable the plotter to draw lines of varying thicknesses without the need to change pens.

Once an architect's practice has decided to make use of a computer aided design and drawing system, a decision has to be made as to the method of operation. It may not be feasible to treat it as a resource, like a photocopier, which anyone can use as and when required, although this could sometimes happen. It is more likely that the computer equipment will be housed in a separate room, with one or more computer operators working under the direction of a CAD section head or manager. These staff should not be isolated from other staff members. Often a CAD operator will be considered to be a member of a specific group in the office and produce all the computer work needed by that group.

A further potential benefit of a CAD system is that the data produced by the computer can be sent electronically down the telephone line to some other office, such as the quantity surveyor's or the contractor's office in a matter of minutes, although at the present time this facility does not seem to be widely used.

8.10 Storage of drawings

However drawings are produced, they will need to be stored for easy access during the course of the project. Drawings should be filed flat and not folded or rolled. Traditionally this is achieved by use of plan chests, but specially designed cabinets are also available which permit drawings to be stored vertically.

Separate drawers will generally be allocated for various types of the architect's own drawings, as well as those produced by other members of the design team – e.g. consulting engineers and sub-contractors. Negatives should be kept separate from prints.

Drawings which are out of date, due to the issue of revised drawings, should either be destroyed, or if they need to be retained for record purposes they should be clearly marked with the word 'superseded'.

Information on the storage of record drawings for completed projects, including microfilming, is given in Section 5.14 of Chapter 5.

8.11 Schedules

Schedules are tabulated statements of information. In their simplest form they consist of a list of items, but more frequently the information is contained within a network of lined boxes.

Schedules have the merit of providing information in a form which can be easily checked. They are also useful for easy ordering of components and materials. Schedules are commonly used to record information on items such as doors and windows, ironmongery, lintels, finishes, colour schemes, manholes and inspection chambers.

8.12 Specifications

A specification is a written document which describes all the work to be carried out, including the quality of the work and the standard of workmanship. It gives a good general view of the work involved but is also able to set out some things in a more detailed way than is possible with notes on drawings.

In the case of new buildings the specification is frequently incorporated into the bills of quantities as a preamble to the bill. Where there is no BQ, the specification will be a separate document. The contractual implication of this, is that if there are no bills of quantities, the specification becomes a contract document.

8.13 Traditional specification

This type of specification gives the full details as to what is required, including the exact method of construction. The specification is generally divided into sections, starting with 'Preliminaries', followed by various trades such as 'Excavations', 'Concrete Work', 'Brickwork and Blockwork'. Information is given about the material and workmanship under the same section.

8.14 NBS

NBS stands for the National Building Specification and uses the CI/SfB coding system. It provides details of the materials under the heading 'Commodities', with the 'Workmanship' items grouped under a separate heading. A collection of standard clauses are provided which can be used for any specification.

The idea behind using the CI/SfB coding system is to facilitate cross referencing between all project documents, as well as with general trade literature. The NBS was originally published by the National Economic Council, and is now published by the RIBA. The arrangement of the various sections follows the SMM system. (See Section 8.17 of this chapter).

8.15 Performance specification

This method of specification writing is more likely to be used for sending to a supplier of components – e.g. doors. It consists of a detailed statement of requirements defined by the level of achievement required. In other words it states what is needed in terms of performance, rather than how the need is to be met, as with a traditional specification. Using a door as an example, a traditional specification would not only give the size of the door, but would also give a full description of the construction and the type of materials to be used both for the core and facings. A performance specification would give the size, and requirements in terms of appearance, but would then go on to define what is required in terms of strength, sound insulation, fire resistance, spread of flame etc.

8.16 Bills of quantities

The bills of quantities (BQ) is a document containing all the items of materials and labour necessary to construct the building. A full description is given of the quality of materials and the standard of workmanship required. The general conditions under which the work is to be done is stated, together with all preliminaries.

The bills of quantities are generally prepared by quantity surveyors and quantity surveying technicians. They are used by contractors to price the work shown on drawings and described in specifications.

The value of the BQ is generally considered to be as follows:

(a) All contractors tender under identical conditions, which is a fairer arrangement.

(b) There is less chance of misunderstandings during the course of the work.

(c) If changes are necessary there is likely to be an agreed rate for pricing the variation.

(d) It assists in agreed payments by stages.

(e) It saves the expense of each contractor preparing his own BQ.

8.17 Method of measurement

The method of measurement generally used – e.g. whether concrete is described in metres cube, or metres square of a certain thickness – is the Standard Method of Measurement (SMM). It is issued by the RICS and being a standard and widely accepted and used document enables the contractor to price the work in accordance with recognised conventions. It is prepared by the RICS and BEC with the blessing of the RIBA.

It means that bills of quantities are nearly always set out in a standard way – that is to say the general format is the same for every job. It also ensures that the work is set out in accordance with the JCT Standard Forms of Building Contracts.

8.18 Preparation of the BQ

Traditionally bills of quantities are prepared in a number of stages. Firstly 'taking off' measurements from the drawings and entering them on dimension paper. Then 'squaring' the dimensions to provide, e.g., metres square of brickwork and metres cube of concrete; transferring them to abstract paper, and 'casting' or adding like dimensions together. The final stage is 'billing' the information into the familiar form of bills of quantities. However with the advent of computers it is becoming common practice to feed the descriptions and dimensions into a computer, which undertakes all the calculations and produces a complete print out of the bills.

8.19 Nominated sub-contractors

Architects need to make decisions on key elements of the building, such as the structural frame, in the early stages of a project. This fact has led to the emergence of nominated sub-contractors.

A nominated sub-contractor is a person or company named by the architect to be responsible for carrying out part of the work – e.g. the structural steelwork.

This puts them in a special relationship with the architect. In the case of structural steelwork for example, it could mean that the nominated sub-contractor could undertake some, or even all, of the steelwork design. However once the contractor has accepted the architect's nomination, and the sub-contract is signed, the relationship is the usual one of contractor and sub-contractor.

The fact that nominated sub-contractors are appointed at an early stage will generally mean that the client will need to be involved. The architect will need to analyse the information on the quotations received from the sub-contractors, so that he can make a recommendation to the client as to why a particular quotation should be accepted.

There are various questions the architect can ask, to help him decide which sub-contractor to recommend. They are:

(a) Has the sub-contractor been used before and was he reliable?

(b) Do the materials and workmanship meet the architect's precise requirements?

(c) Do the materials and workmanship meet all statutory requirements, BSSs and CPs?

(d) Are the programme dates which are offered acceptable?

(e) Is the quoted price competitive?

(f) Is the quoted price unambiguous? What, if any, discounts are offered?

(g) What are the terms of payment?

There is a standard procedure for formalizing the appointment of a sub-contractor. The documents used and the procedure followed are summarised below. It may seem a 'long winded' system but experience has shown it is worth adopting.

Documents Used

Tender NCS/1
This tender form, addressed to the employer and main contractor, is approved by the architect on behalf of the employer and accepted by the main contractor. It gives the amount of the sub-contract as well as other details such as the daywork rates, certificate periods and retention amount.

Agreement NSC/2
This agreement is between the sub-contractor and employer stating that the sub-contractor will be appointed for sub-contract work as part of the main contract which has yet to be let. It confirms that the architect has approved the sub-contractor's tender and intends to nominate the sub-contractor, provided agreement can be reached between the main contractor and sub-contractor on the sub-contract conditions.

Nomination NSC/3
This nomination form, from the architect to the main contractor, nominates the sub-contractor for a specific contract.

Sub-contract NSC/4
This sub-contract is made and signed between the main contractor and sub-contractor, and is related to the sub-contractor's Tender NSC1.

Order of procedure

(a) The architect prepares Tender NSC/1 and Agreement NSC/2 and sends them to the sub-contractor.

(b) The sub-contractor completes and signs Tender NSC/1 and signs Agreement NSC/2 and returns them to the architect.

(c) The architect signs his approval of Tender NSC/1 on behalf of the employer, and the employer signs the Agreement NSC/2. The architect and the sub-contractor are given a copy of the Agreement NSC/2.

(d) The architect sends the main contractor copies of Tender NSC/1 and Agreement NSC/2. The contractor checks Schedule 1 of Tender NSC/1 and completes part of Schedule 2 as necessary. He signs Tender NSC/1 and returns it to the architect.

(e) The architect sends the Tender NSC/1 and Nomination NSC/3 to the main contractor, with a copy to the sub-contractor.

(f) The main contractor and the sub-contractor enter into the Sub-contract NSC/4.

An alternative method which may be followed is just to use the sub-contract NSC/4a, with the option to also use the Agreement NSC/2a.

8.20 Building Regulations of 1985

The main purpose of the Building Regulations is to ensure minimum standard of health and safety of all people who are in or about buildings. They also deal with the conservation of fuel and power, and facilities for disabled people. Details of the requirements of the Building Regulations were previously discussed in Section 7.8 of Chapter 7.

Most buildings and building work require permission under the Building Regulations, but the following work is exempt:

(a) Buildings controlled under other legislation – e.g. a building subject to the Explosive Acts.

(b) Buildings not frequented by people – e.g. a detached building, housing fixed plant or machinery.

(c) Greenhouses and agricultural buildings.

(d) Temporary buildings and mobile homes.

(e) Ancillary buildings – e.g. a building used only by people engaged in construction during the course of that work.

(f) Small detached buildings with a total floor area of not more than 30 square metres, and with no sleeping accommodation.

The regulations do apply to extensions to buildings, apart from greenhouses, conservatories, car ports open on two sides, or covered yards with an area not exceeding 30 square metres. They also apply to certain changes of use.

There are two alternative systems of building control, and a choice has to be made between the local authority or a private approved inspector. At the present time, possibly due to problems with obtaining suitable professional indemnity insurance, private approved inspectors do not appear to be widely used.

If application is made to the local authority, the applicant can, except in the case of shops or offices, either give a Building Notice supported by a site plan, or else deposit a full set of plans. If the applicant just gives a Building Notice and a site plan, the local authority may ask for more drawings to help them with their inspection role.

In either case a prescribed fee has to be paid, and the local authority must be given at least 48 hours notice before work starts. The amount of fee payable depends on the size and type of project. The main categories are small domestic buildings, multiple schemes (e.g. a terrace of houses); small garages and alterations, and other work.

The main advantage of initially submitting 'full plans' is that once they are approved, the building can be constructed in accordance with these plans, with the confidence that the local authority will be satisfied with the result.

If the application is made to a private approved inspector, the inspector and the applicant must jointly give the local authority an Initial Notice, a site plan, description of the works, including drainage details, together with evidence that an approved scheme of insurance applies to the work. Work cannot start until the Initial Notice has been accepted or ten days have passed without it being rejected. The work then has to be done to the satisfaction of the inspector. If the applicant wishes, he can submit detailed plans to the inspector and ask him to provide a Plans Certificate certifying that the plans comply with the building regulations. On completion of the work the inspector will issue a Final Certificate.

The private approved inspector must generally be independent of the builder and designer, but there is an exception to this general rule in the case of alterations or extension work to one or two storey houses.

The need for structural and 'U' value calculations can be dispensed with by submitting a certificate from an approved qualified engineer or designer.

Responsibility for ensuring adequate drainage provision and building work over sewers is under the control of the local authority.

There is provision for dispensing and relaxing the regulations in appropriate cases. A Relaxation can be given by the local authority in respect of Part B1 Means of Escape; Part L2 and L3 Conservation of Fuel and Power; and Schedule 2 Facilities for Disabled People. Lower standards of performance may be accepted in each case.

A Dispensation can be given by the local authority in respect of Regulation 7 Materials and Workmanship; Part A: Structure; Parts B2, B3, B4: Fire protection; Part C: Site protection and resistance to moisture; Part D: Toxic substances; Part E: Sound resistance; Part F: Ventilation; Part G: Hygiene; Part H: Drainage; Part J: Heat producing appliances; and Part K: Staircases and ramps. In such cases the local authority may agree that a particular regulation does not need to apply at all.

If the local authority rejects the plans submitted to them under the building regulations, an application can be made to the Secretary of State for a ruling on the specific requirements of the local authority. This is known as a determination. A fee is payable – the amount depends on the size of the project.

If the local authority considers a building has been erected which does not conform with the regulations, they can serve a notice requiring it to be altered or pulled down so that it does conform.

8.21 Town planning acts

The purpose of town planning acts, is to ensure that all buildings are of an acceptable appearance; are appropriate to their surroundings; and in town planning parlance will not be 'detrimental to the amenities of the area', or 'against the public interest'.

Permission is required for most buildings. There are exemptions given to certain small developments, including extensions to semi-detached and detached houses of not more than 70 metres cube or 15%, whichever is greater, up to 115 metres cube, and extensions to industrial buildings by 25% of volume and up to 1000 metres square of floor space.

To obtain planning permission, application must be made to the planning department of the district council. The architect normally acts as the employer's agent. The usual procedure is to have an initial discussion with the town planning officer (or borough development officer) and to look at the structure plan and zoning for the area, to decide whether planning permission is likely to be given.

Dependent on these preliminary enquiries, a decision can be made as to whether to apply for Outline Planning Permission – i.e. permission in principle to erect the building – or Full Planning Permission. In most cases a detailed application from the outset is probably the best way to proceed.

If outline permission is to be sought, the following information is required:

Four copies of the application forms, generally consisting of Part 1 for all applicants, plus Part 2 for industrial, office and shop developments, giving additional details of traffic, parking etc.

One copy of a certificate confirming the situation regarding ownership of the land.

One copy of a block plan indicating the position of the development.

If full permission is sought, information is required as for outline permission, plus the following:

Four copies of every floor plan.

Four copies of every elevation.

The decision of the application rests with the Local Authority Planning Committee, with guidance from professional planning officers. They generally meet once a month throughout the year. Minor developments – e.g. house extensions – may be determined by the local authority planning officers. These are called 'delegated decisions'. Decisions are generally made within eight weeks and a Decision Notice is sent to the applicant.

If outline permission is obtained, full permission has then to be obtained within three years. If full permission is obtained, work on site must start within five years. If permission is refused, on either an outline or full application, an appeal can be made to the Secretary of State for the Environment.

Fees are payable to the planning authority when applications are made. The amount varies according to the type of application and the type of development.

Sometimes planning permission is only granted subject to planning conditions. A planning condition is a requirement which can be properly imposed to meet the objectives of planning policies relevant to the proposed development. The planning conditions must be fair, reasonable, and relevant to the proposals concerned. For example while it would be considered reasonable for a developer to include enough car parking spaces to cater for people occupying the new buildings, it would be unreasonable also to expect him to provide sufficient spaces to meet the needs of a nearby local authority recreational facility.

Applicants can appeal against a planning condition which a local authority is seeking to impose. The appeal is made initially to the local authority, but if this is refused an appeal can then be made to the Secretary of State, and ultimately to the courts on a point of law. Section 7.9 of Chapter 7 includes an outline as to how the town planning acts provide a constraining effect on the architect.

8.22 Other acts

Buildings may also be affected by various other acts. Space does not allow for all of these acts to be covered in detail. In fact they would require a book of their own to do so. However, four of the more important ones are outlined below.

Health and safety at Work Act of 1974

This act covers the working conditions of everyone, so that if the building that the architect is designing will be a place of work he must make sure that conditions in the completed building will meet the requirements of the act. Formal approval is not given, but it is a reasonable procedure for the architect to show his drawings to the Health and Safety at Work Act inspector and obtain his informal approval of the scheme. The act is linked to the Factory Acts and the Shops and Offices Acts.

Fire Precautions Acts of 1971

A fire certificate needs to be obtained from the local fire authority for certain classes of buildings – e.g. places of amusement; educational establishments; residential establishments such as hotels, hostels and old peoples homes. The main emphasis is directed towards the safety of the occupants in case of fire, including a safe means of escape.

Clean Air Act of 1968

This is operated by the local authority and governs things such as the height of chimneys and the emission of fumes.

Highways Acts

These are operated by the highway authority and deal with matters such as road improvements and building lines.

8.23 Insurance

Insurance of a building is not a statutory requirement, but the architect needs to remember that the client will almost certainly want to insure the building. This may not be possible unless the insurers are satisfied that the building does not constitute a fire risk. In the case of a large complex building, the architect will often meet with the insurers to agree his scheme before it is finalised.

9

Pre-contract procedures generally

9.1 Introduction

The first main part of a building project is the pre-contract period, from the moment a client first approaches the architect, with his requirements, to the time when the main contract and sub-contracts have been signed.

This is covered by Stages A to J of the RIBA Plan of Work, and the full procedure is explained in the RIBA Job Book.

It should be emphasised again that the RIBA Plan of Work is an invaluable guide to the way the architect arranges his work, but it is a flexible and not a rigid pattern of work. In practice there will, at times, be an overlap between the various stages, and changes in the order of the various operations.

Detailed bills of quantities will always be prepared during the pre-contract stage, as these are required for tendering purposes. Detailed specifications are also required for the same purpose.

The exact extent of the drawings prepared will vary from contract to contract. Ideally every drawing the contractor needs to complete the project will also be produced at the pre-contract stage, but on large, complicated jobs this is seldom practicable. The amount of information provided will depend to a great extent on the contractual form used, but an indication on the information provided for tendering is given later in this chapter – see Section 9.5.

9.2 Communicating design outcomes

The architect has the task of producing a design which will, in his professional judgement, completely satisfy his client's brief. Having done this, he has the task of presenting his design solution to the client.

There are a variety of methods he can use, and the choice will be influenced by the type, size and value of the project. The architect will generally aim to achieve a good standard of presentation, both as a matter of professional pride, and also in an attempt to impress the client, and others such as the planning authority, on the attractiveness of the design.

The architect should remember that many lay-people have great difficulty in understanding drawings, so a perspective is most helpful in portraying the appearance of the building. Models are especially useful and a good way to explain and 'sell' the project. Laymen may understand plans, but to most people of a non-technical background, sections tend to be something of a mystery. On a small project, such as a house, the architect will generally provide floor plans and a perspective.

For a building to be erected on a site in an urban area between existing buildings, the perspective should show the surrounding buildings. One method is to produce a perspective, which is a combination of a drawing of the proposed building, arranged with photographs of the existing buildings. It can then be re-photographed to give a realistic impression as to how the proposed buildings will relate to the existing buildings.

On an industrial complex a model showing the inter-relationship of new and existing buildings is very helpful. The model does not have to be expensive, as often a simple 'block' model, without a lot of detail, will be adequate.

On the larger, more costly projects, it is worth spending time and money on a more elaborate presentation. A detailed model will be expected, perhaps showing important parts of the internal layout. If a formal presentation is required – e.g. to a board of directors – it is worth preparing photographic slides of all models, internal and external perspectives, views of the site, plans and other drawings, so that the scheme can be presented in an orderly fashion, with an appropriate commentary.

The architect also needs to communicate his intentions to specialist members of the design team, and others. As was stated in the previous chapter, he needs to remember that each person, to some extent, requires different information. They all use drawings as the normal means of communication. The architect will generally use this means of relaying his design intentions, but he will tailor his drawings to suit the needs of individual members of the building team. This will often be achieved by making negative copies of the basic drawings, and adding information specifically to suit different people.

9.3 Approximate estimates

As the cost of any job is so important, particularly to the client, approximate estimates are expected to be provided at the various pre-contract stages of the project. Unfortunately these are often a 'bone of contention', especially when events prove them to be inaccurate. Nevertheless they are the basis on which the client will instruct the architect to proceed with his work.

When presenting an estimate it is important to clarify the date to which it is linked – e.g. does it refer to the date it is given to the client; the date the job is expected to start; or is it the actual cost of the completed building? Clearly, with inflation to be contended with, the three estimates based on these three dates, probably separated by several years, are likely to be significantly different.

It is also important to state clearly what is included in an estimate, and what is excluded.

The architect will of course generally remind his client that, until the detailed drawings have been prepared and priced, the estimate can of necessity only be approximate. Nevertheless if the tender price is dramatically more than the first approximate estimate, the client is likely to lose confidence in his architect, and may even consider abandoning the project.

There are various types of approximate estimates and some of the most common are listed below.

Cost per unit of accommodation

For example, the price per bed for a hospital; per scholar for a school; per seat for a church, theatre or cinema; and per room for a block of flats, the unit cost provides an almost immediate method of putting a 'price tag' on a larger building. However, unless the figures are based on similar buildings, they can only be taken as very approximate. To produce the approximate cost using this method, all that is required is for the client to state how many beds/scholars/ seats/rooms etc., are required, so that the architect or QS, using a unit cost derived from previous, similar jobs, can prepare an estimate by making a simple calculation.

Cost per square metre of floor area

This is a quick and easily adjustable method, but it takes no account of heights, complexity, or plan shape of the building. Again with this method an approximate cost can be produced without the need for any drawings. The client will have to supply a schedule of room areas to which the architect will add areas the client may have omitted, such as circulation spaces, toilets etc. This will give an overall floor area, which can be multiplied by a price per square metre, derived from previous jobs. However, if the project is sufficiently advanced for sketch plans to have been prepared, the floor area, and hence the estimate, can be calculated with greater accuracy.

Cost per metre cube of building

This is also a fairly quick method, but as it is generally used to provide an overall figure for the volume of the building, it takes no account of different room heights and uses within different parts of the building. Again, it is theoretically possible to produce an estimate before any drawings have been prepared, by calculating the total floor area, as described under the previous section 'cost per square metre of floor area', and then multiplying it by an assumed average storey height, to arrive at the cubic capacity of the building. However, in practice this method is more likely to be used when both plans and sections are available, so that the cubic capacity can be calculated with a greater degree of accuracy.

Cost per element of building

For elements such as floors, walls, roof etc., this method provides a more accurate estimate, but takes longer to prepare, and sketch plans, elevations, and sections are required. Each element, including finishes, is priced according to a unit rate per square metre.

In addition to the above methods, at the later stages of the design process, the quantity surveyor may take off approximate quantities to arrive at a more accurate estimate.

9.4 Concept of tendering

The concept of traditional, competitive tendering is to present the client (employer) with comparable prices obtained from a number of different contractors. This is achieved by the design team, acting on behalf of the client, sending all competing contractors identical information – i.e. bills of quantities, drawings, schedules and specifications – on which they can base their tenders.

A system of open tendering may be used, in which any firm wishing to compete is allowed to submit a tender. The open system has its disadvantages. As far as the contractors are concerned it involves them in a large amount of work, with only a limited chance of success, as they are likely to be in competition with a large number of firms. The danger to the client is that if everyone is allowed to join the competition, it is less likely they will all be of equal standing and reliability.

A system of selected, or closed, tendering, is often preferred, and in this system the architect, generally with the help of the quantity surveyor, and the agreement of the client, prepares a list of contractors who will be invited to tender. As a rule, the invited firms are known to the architect or QS, but sometimes they are selected from contractors who respond to an advertisement in the local or technical press.

The number of firms who should be invited to tender is a matter of opinion, but some architects and quantity surveyors set the figure at between four and eight, depending on the size and type of the job. In preparing the list of tenderers it is important to ensure, as far as possible, that they are all capable of undertaking the work to the required standard and time scale.

The architect will, on a project of any importance, prepare his list of tenderers about three months before the work is due to commence on the site. This is because a number of processes are involved, and they each take time to complete. The client has to be consulted; a check has to be made that all the firms on the list wish to tender; the documents have to be assembled and dispatched; the contractors need time to prepare their tenders; the submitted tenders have to be analysed; and the successful contractor will require time to prepare for starting work on site – i.e. a 'lead-in' time.

Sufficient time must be allowed for contractors to prepare their tenders – generally at least four weeks unless the project is a very small, uncomplicated one. It is worth mentioning that, particularly with selected tendering, it is good practice to award the contract to the firm who submits the lowest tender. Clearly an architect who acts otherwise will soon lose credibility with contractors whose prices were the lowest, but who were not given the jobs. The legal position is discussed in Section 9.6 of this chapter.

Although selective tendering is a well established system, offering the client reliable information on the cost of the project, and the satisfaction of knowing that the selective price is competitive, it is not the only available method. A strong case can be made out for involving the contractor in the project at the design stage, mainly on the grounds that design cannot be divorced from the construction process. If the contractor's expertise is utilised in respect of economic constructional techniques, the best use of proprietary components, and the appropriate utilisation of sub-contracting skills, the architect is more likely to design a building which can be built more easily, quickly, and at less cost. It is also often true that, if a building is easier to build, the workmanship is likely to be better. Certainly it is true to say that, if the design team can produce the sort of details which mean that the craftsman needs three pairs of hands to construct them, the quality of work is likely to suffer.

Early involvement of the contractor, often leads to an early start by the contractor, particularly if a start is made before all drawings are completed. This should mean that the project will also be completed earlier, and the client will gain an earlier financial benefit from his investment.

The adoption of a system of nominating a single contractor at an early stage places an additional responsibility on both the architect and quantity surveyor. The architect must take care to select a thoroughly reliable contractor, who can make a positive contribution to the project if brought in at the design stage. The QS will have a major role in ensuring that an effective system of cost control is established, and that the nominated contractor does not overcharge the client for the work.

Standard forms and letters which may be used for the tendering procedure are shown in Chapter 13.

9.5 Information for tendering

The following information will normally be sent to contractors who are invited to tender for a project.

(a) Bills of quantities: two copies.

(b) Specification, if not an integral part of the BQ: one copy.

(c) Drawings: one set, typically containing the following:
   (i)   Block plan locating the site.
   (ii) Site plan, locating the position and extent of buildings, roads/pavings, services, fences etc.
   (iii) Floor plans, sections and elevations, showing the location of all spaces, elements, and materials, including the following:
        Demolitions.
        Excavations and earthworks.
        Foundation arrangement, including piling and underpinning work.
        Concrete work, including positions and general profiles of all slabs, beams, walls, columns, and staircases.
        Steel frames, including positions of beams and columns.
        Brickwork and blockwork, including positions of all openings, piers, special features etc.
        Wall panels.
        Finishes to all walls, floors, ceilings and roofs, clearly defining position and extent of each finish.
        Tanking to basement and other areas, and other special waterproofing treatments.
        Glazing.
        Painting.
        Services, with routes of ducts, pipes and cables.

(d) Assembly drawings, to clarify unusual details, or items which cannot be adequately described in the BQ or specification.

(e) Component drawings, including the following items:
    Windows and curtain walling.
    Doors and shutters.
    Rooflights.
    Preformed staircases, ladders, and balustrades.
    Duct covers.
    Built in fittings.

(f) Information: For example, loadings – these are required for the contractor's temporary works items, such as formwork and cranage.

(g) Forms of tender: two copies.

(h) Addressed envelope for the return of the tender.

(j) Covering letter sent out with the documents, and containing the following information:
    (i)   List of enclosures.
    (ii) Time, date, and place for the return of tenders.
    (iii) Details of when, how, and where, additional drawings to those sent to the tenderers can be inspected.
    (iv) Arrangements for inspecting the site.
    (v)   Time, date and place where the tenders will be opened, and whether contractors may be present. *NB*: Generally this will not be permitted.
    (vi) A request for contractors to acknowledge the safe receipt of all the documents.

9.6 Architect's responsibility towards tenderers

It is a long established practice when inviting contractors to tender, to state that no guarantee is given to accept the lowest, or any of the tenders, submitted. At 'the invitation to tender' stage the architect is therefore under no legal obligation to any of the contractors who are tendering.

An obligation arises when a contract situation occurs, due to both parties accepting an agreement, i.e. when an offer made by one party (the contractor) is accepted by the other party (the employer).

When a contractor submits a tender, he is deemed to have made a firm offer to build a specific building, for a stated price, in a stated period of time. The contractor may, when submitting his tender, add conditions on the form of tender sent to him, and they will become part of his tender offer. If the architect, acting on behalf of the employer, accepts this tender offer, a binding contract takes place. If the architect objects to the conditions which the contractor has added to his tender offer, there is no binding contract. This is in accord with one of the principles of a binding contract, that the parties to the contract must reach an agreement.

The translating of the contract into a written agreement should be a matter of form, once the architect, acting for the employer, has given an unqualified acceptance of the contractor's tender offer.

After the tenders have been received, the architect, generally with the help of the quantity surveyor, will check that the contractor has not made any errors in pricing the bills of quantities. If a serious mistake has been made, the architect is under an obligation to draw the contractor's attention to the error, and give him the opportunity to remedy the situation. The procedure for doing this is discussed in Section 10.9 of Chapter 10.

If the architect fails to draw the contractor's attention to errors, he may find himself sued by the contractor. This situation arose in a case which came before the courts in 1955 – Dutton vs Louth Corporation. The contractor claimed that the architect misled him into signing a contract, because he (the architect) had noticed an error of £100,000 in the contractor's priced bills of quantities, but had not drawn the contractor's attention to it. At the original hearing the contractor won his action against the architect and the Corporation, but the judgement was subsequently reversed by the Court of Appeal. The grounds for this reversal was that, although the architect had not drawn the contractor's attention to the particular error of £100,000, he had given a general warning to the contractor that there were serious errors in his bills of quantities.

Pre-contract procedures stages

10.1 Introduction

This chapter deals with the nine stages included in the RIBA Plan of Work which take place before operations commence on site. They are:

Stage A: Inception.
Stage B: Feasibility.
Stage C: Outline proposals.
Stage D: Scheme design.
Stage E: Detail design.
Stage F: Production information.
Stage G: Bills of quantities.
Stage H: Tender action.
Stage J: Project planning.

Although the RIBA Plan of Work is used as the basis for the order in which architects undertake their various tasks, both during the pre-contract stages (discussed in Chapters 9 and 10) and in the contract-stages (discussed in Chapters 11 and 12) it is only used as a framework. It is not important that listed items are always rigidly included in their suggested stage. Sometimes tasks will be done at a different stage to that listed, or a number of tasks will be combined together, or there will be overlapping of stages. The main thing for students to remember is that the architect must work in a logical and systematic way, and make sure that all decisions and instructions are properly recorded.

During the pre-contract stages various letters will be written, and agendas for meetings and other documents prepared. Some examples of these are included in Chapter 13. They relate to a project for a factory, for the assembly of electronic components, together with a two-storey office block.

10.2 Stage A – Inception

At this stage the client approaches the architect for her professional assistance. The architect agrees to help her and establishes the terms of her appointment and the client's requirements.

The architect has to undertake the following tasks.

(a) Check it is possible to accept the job. This includes satisfying herself the client is genuine and has the resources to finance the project; making sure that no other architects are involved, and that she has the resources to meet the client's needs.

(b) Agree the terms of the appointment. This includes responsibilities, fees, employment of the QS and other consultants, and channels of communications.

(c) Obtain initial details of the client's requirements and of the site.

(d) Initiate office procedures. This will include opening files, a job book, fees and other records, and deciding how the architect will organise her part of the job and who will be involved.

A job directory will be prepared in which the names, addresses and telephone numbers of the client, his representatives, the various consultants, and any other interested parties will be entered.

At least one meeting with the client will be necessary. The architect will probably avoid seeking too much detail from the client at this stage, but will aim to establish the general nature of her requirements, together with the location of the site and some detail. The information obtained can be recorded on a Briefing Check List. (See Fig. 13.1).

Agreement will need to be obtained on the terms of the architect's appointment, together with details of the fees. These will generally be charged at a percentage of the cost of the project, with the exact percentage dependent on the type of job. A schedule of fees will normally be prepared ready for completing during the various stages of the job. A chart recording resources to be allocated to the job, with performance targets will also generally be prepared. It is important for the architect to plan his part of the work in such a way that he completes it within the total amount of his fees.

At this stage the main financial concern of the architect will be to establish cost limitations. The architect may mention typical costs per square metre of floor area, but all figures should be quoted with reservations, and it is best, if possible, to leave this matter until Stage B – Feasibility.

The tender procedure will also need to be discussed, together with the form of contract to be used, and decisions regarding the appointment of nominated sub-contractors and suppliers.

The architect will inform the client of approvals required under planning, building and other regulations, giving him details as to how this will affect the pre-contract programme, and what fees are payable.

Agreement will have to be made as to who will be acting for the client. If the project is anything more complicated than a simple building, such as a house, with only the intending owner/occupier involved, a decision will need to be made as to which members of the client's staff will have power to act for him. Similarly there is a need to know which members of the architect's staff will be involved in the project, and what authority each of them will have.

It is clearly important that satisfactory methods of communications be established in the initial stages of the job. The architect will often advise the client on the best way of setting up communications with the design team, including defining individual responsibilities, and methods of giving and receiving instructions.

The procedures for the next stages of the project will generally be discussed with the client, and in particular his agreement will be obtained, to meeting any charges likely to be incurred, such as trial holes or boreholes dug as part of the site investigation.

Everything which is agreed at the initial meeting should be comfirmed in writing. A typical letter sent by the architect to the client after such an initial meeting is shown in Fig. 13.2. This will generally be followed by the signing of an appropriate 'Memorandum of Agreement'.

10.3 Stage B – Feasibility

At this stage the architect will establish whether it is technically possible to construct the building the client requires on the available site. In undertaking this appraisal the architect will have to obtain the following details.

(a) Additional information on the client's requirements to that provided at Stage A – Inception.

(b) Detailed information on the site.

(c) Information from 'third parties' who may be involved with the proposed building.

(d) Information on costs.

The way in which the architect obtains the detailed information from the client will vary according to the particular job. In the case of a house it will probably entail a meeting with the client, at which the client will provide details as to who will occupy the house, detailing the life style of the occupants, and confirming how much money it is possible to spend on the project. In some cases the client may spell out in detail the size, location and appearance of all the rooms required, and even take the architect around houses containing features he would like incorporated in the proposed house.

In the case of an industrialist requiring a factory, the architect will need to obtain details of the manufacturing process, which may involve visits to the client's other factories, and detailed meetings with the industrialist's staff.

Certainly a job of any complexity will require more information than the outline details obtained at the previous stage, and illustrated in the typical Briefing Checklist. (See Fig. 13.1). Part of the Detailed Briefing document is shown in Fig. 13.3. This more detailed brief will include information such as sizes, function and spatial relationships of all rooms and areas, including details of services and finishes to walls, floors and ceilings.

In order to obtain information on the site there will need to be a site investigation. As an aid to this task, architects will often use standard site investigation report forms. (See Fig. 13.5). A standard check list is also often used by architects for surveying buildings which are part of a building project. As well as looking at the site and writing down what he sees, the architect will need to survey the site to establish the plan size, details and contours. He will also need to arrange for trial holes to be dug or boreholes to be drilled to establish the nature of the subsoil.

One of the most important 'third parties' involved in the scheme will be the local authority planning department. The architect will normally have an informal meeting with the responsible planning officer to establish whether planning permission is likely to be given. If at this meeting, for example, the planning officer states it is most unlikely that permission will be given to build a house, as that particular site is in an area zoned for industrial use, the architect may decide it is not worthwhile proceeding with the scheme. A standard Briefing Check List is often used to record information obtained from the local authority. (See Fig. 13.6).

Meetings may also take place with the highway authority to check there are no problems relating to access into the site, and confirmation will be obtained from the statutory undertakings, such as water, gas and electricity companies that all the services the client requires for his building are available.

At the conclusion of all his investigations and enquiries the architect will then be able to report back to the client, to state whether or not it is a feasible proposition to build a building of the type the client requires, on the site in question. Sometimes the answer will be a 'straight yes'. At other times the architect will report that it is possible to build a building to meet the client's needs, but it would have to be in a different form to that originally envisaged.

In any event the architect will also include a preliminary cost appraisal to check that it is also feasible to provide the type of building the client wants for the amount of money he has to spend. It should be emphasised that any estimates given will be 'very approximate', based possibly on a square metre price, linked to a schedule of accommodation and room areas. Often cost studies of alternative solutions to the one originally discussed with the client may be prepared, if this is thought to be in the client's interest.

The form of the Feasibility Report will depend on the size, type and importance of the project. On a very small job, it may consist of little more than a long letter. On a large important job it will include drawings, perhaps a model, details of people involved, information on the site, design constraints, cost appraisals, the anticipated programme, together with schedules of the accommodation and room areas.

At Stage B the architect will also need to confirm the appointment of the quantity surveyor, engineer and other consultants, and prepare for the next stage of the project.

The design team needs to be organised, with the roles of the members clearly defined, and relationships between the design team and client's representatives established.

10.4 Stage C – Outline proposals

At this stage the architect, with the help of other members of the design team, will carefully analyse the client's requirements. He will relate these requirements to the information obtained at Stage B – Feasibility, from the site investigation and other sources. Any further information needed from members of the client's organisation will be obtained, and studies will be made of circulation and other problems, and alternative design solution considered.

Expert advice will be obtained from the various consultants on the structural, building engineering services, and cost aspects. Account will be taken of all the constraints disclosed during this stage and previous ones.

Having collected together all the relevant information, and considered the various alternatives, the architect, with other members of the design team, will decide in outline, the best design solution, and prepare the outline scheme drawings.

The QS will consider the cost limits of the project, and the architect will help him in this assessment as required. The QS will probably translate the cost limits of the project into a price of so much a square metre for each building included in the project. The architect will discuss with the QS what standard of building can be provided within these limits.

An outline pre-contract programme will be prepared so as to give the client an indication as to when the building work will commence on site, and how long it will take to complete. It is important that the client realises, that between the time he instructs the architect to act for him, and the time when building work commences on site, there are a number of processes which have to be undertaken. If any of these processes take longer than anticipated this will delay the starting date for building work. For example, if the client says he will give a decision to proceed within a week of receiving the scheme design from the architect but actually takes a month to make up his mind, this will delay the job by three weeks. If an architect just gives the client a date when the job will start, without the back up of a programme, it is likely the client

Table 10.1 Pre-contract bar chart programme

LANE & RALPH

PRE-CONTRACT PROGRAMME   DATE: 23RD MAY 1988

PROJECT: FACTORY AND OFFICE BLOCK, STEPHEN'S INDUSTRIAL ESTATE
             BOX HILL

ACTIVITY	YEAR											Week ending										
	APRIL		MAY				JUNE				JULY				AUGUST				SEPTEMBER			
	23	30	7	14	21	28	4	11	18	25	2	9	16	23	30	6	13	20	27	3	10	17	24
Outline sketch drawings	▨																						
Scheme design drawings			▨▨▨																				
Consideration and approval by client						▨																	
Statutory approvals								▨▨▨															
Detail design drawings							▨																
Working (production) drawings										▨▨▨▨▨▨▨▨▨▨▨▨												
Specifications								▨▨▨															
Consultant's design and drawings									▨▨▨▨													
Sub-contractors quotations											▨▨												
Bills of quantities													▨▨▨										
Printing of bills of quantities																	▨						
Tendering period																			▨▨				
Receipt and decision on tenders																							▨
HAND OVER SITE TO CONTRACTOR																	17TH OCTOBER 1988						

will assume the date will remain fixed in spite of anything that happens in the intervening period. Table 10.1 shows a typical pre-contract programme.

There is not necessarily a clear demarcation between the various design and drawing stages. For example detail design drawings, such as 1:100 location plans, elevations and sections, may be used for obtaining the statutory approvals, and will then have some additional information added to them so that they can become part of the set of the production drawings issued to the contract for use on the site. The stage at which some, or all, of the applications for statutory approvals are made will also vary from project to project.

A report will be prepared for consideration by the client. The drawings submitted with this report will, as the name of this stage implies, be in outline only. They may consist of little more than a block layout showing the relationship between the different types of accommodation for each floor, with main dimensions. In other words individual rooms would not be shown. A site plan would normally be provided, showing the position of the buildings on the site, with the location of the services. The written part of the report would indicate the type of structure envisaged; the scope of intended building engineering services, and information on the programme and cost.

At this stage 15% of the fees are now due, so the architect will submit his account to the client, asking for payment.

10.5 Stage D – Scheme design

At this stage, the design team will prepare a scheme design sufficiently detailed, to show the spatial arrangements of the various parts of the building, as well as the appearance of the building, and an indication of the materials used.

In order to do this the architect will need to complete his studies to establish 'user requirements'. If necessary additional visits and investigations will be made to achieve this. The client will be asked to provide any additional information required by the architect. The architect will also check that the client has acquired the site.

In order to organise the design, meetings at which solutions will be discussed and developed will be necessary. Decisions will be made regarding design aspects, materials, finishes, services, contributions by specialist firms, and various other matters.

It is likely that, at this stage application will be made to the local authority for full planning permission, and building regulations approval. There is however no hard and fast rule as to the exact stage when approval is sought. For example, sometimes applications may be delayed until Stage E – Detail design. Generally the same drawings will be used in support of both the planning and building regulations applications.

The information required in support of the planning application was discussed under Section 8.21 of Chapter 8. It will generally be sensible before depositing the application, to have a further informal discussion with the local planning officer, so as to arrive at a solution which has his support. At such a meeting he may suggest that it is likely permission will only be given subject to planning conditions. As has been previously stated, such planning conditions must be fair, reasonable and relevant to the development concerned.

The information required in support of the building regulations application was discussed under Section 8.20 of Chapter 8. Certain work is exempted from building control, and if this appears to be the case for a particular project, the local authority should be approached for their confirmation.

The appropriate fees for both the town planning and building regulation applications will have to be sent to the local authority, along with the relevant forms and drawings.

When considering the application the local authority will check that the bodies responsible for matters such as highways, drainage and safety in the case of fire, are happy with the proposals. This is another reason why it is advisable to consult informally with the local authority before making a submission. They will often be able to advise the architect of other approvals required at this stage. In any event it is sensible to approach everyone likely to be affected. For example if a fire certificate will be required for the completed building, it is best to discover the fire officer's

Table 10.2   Cost plan

COST PLAN	SHEET NO. 2	
PROJECT FACTORY & OFFICE BLOCK, STEPHEN'S INDUSTRIAL ESTATE, BOX HILL		
PART OF PROJECT OFFICE BLOCK		
ELEMENT	**£**	**COST**
Substructure incl. grnd slab	16,000	
Frame	23,000	
Upper floors	8,000	
Stairs	6,000	
Roof	13,000	
External walls	38,000	
External doors / windows	37,000	
Internal walls / partitions	4,000	
Floor finishes	13,000	
Wall finishes	10,000	
Ceiling finishes	11,000	
Fittings	6,000	
Furniture	6,000	
Sanitary appliances	6,000	
Services equipment	—	
External drainage	3,000	
Refuse disposal	—	
Discharge pipework	3,000	
Cold water services	3,000	
Hot water services	7,000	
Heating services	32,000	
Air conditioning services	—	
Gas services	3,000	
Special services	—	
Electrical services	26,000	
Lifts / hoists / conveyers	—	
Fire protection	7,000	
Lightning protection	3,000	
Burglar protection	3,000	
Audio systems	3,000	
Special installations	—	
TOTAL COST (taken to summary)	£290,000	
TOTAL FLOOR AREA	600 SQUARE METRES	
PRICE / SQUARE METRE	£483	
DATE PREPARED	6TH MAY 1988	

requirements at a stage when they can be incorporated in the drawings submitted for planning and building regulations approvals.

An example of part of a planning application form is given in Fig. 13.8, and an example of a building regulation form is given in Fig. 13.9.

The quantity surveyor will prepare a 'cost plan' and the architect will help him as required. This cost plan will indicate to the client the approximate cost, so that he is aware of his financial commitment, and will show how the total cost is allocated among the various parts of the project. Table 10.2 shows part of the cost plan for a project. There will also be a separate sheet for the factory building, again-sub-divided into the various elements, and a sheet for the external works. These three parts of the project will be added together, with a further addition for preliminaries, to give the total cost of the job.

The design team's proposals need to be submitted to the client in an attractive 'presentation' form. As in previous stages the content will depend on the size and importance of the project, but will normally include plans, basic sections, and elevations or perspectives. Sometimes models and photographs will be used. The written part of the submission will, generally include an outline specification, an explanation as to how the client's requirements have been met, outline information on the building engineering services, programme details, and estimated costs.

The scheme design is expected to summarise the client's requirements in respect of accommodation and the general arrangement of the buildings, and he needs to be advised that, once he has approved the scheme, he should not make any changes, unless he is prepared to risk incurring additional costs.

A further 20% of the architect's fees is now due, so the architect will generally submit his account for this amount. Preparations will be made for the next stage of the project, so that the work can proceed in a smooth and orderly manner as soon as the client has approved the scheme design and authorised proceeding to Stage E – Detail design.

10.6 Stage E – Detail design

At the end of the previous stage, the client should have given approval for the pre-contract work on the project to proceed on the basis of the scheme design drawings. It is important that he is aware that any modifications from now on may lead to him incurring extra costs, and a possible delay in the start and completion of the project on site. The client should be politely informed of this fact in writing. A typical letter is shown in Fig. 13.10.

At Stage E the design is developed in a more finalised form, including more detailed drawings and specifications, and incorporating the specialist contributions of the various consultants. The drawings and specifications will form the basis of the production drawings prepared at the next stage.

Once again meetings will take place between the various members of the design team, and where necessary further information will be obtained from the client, mainly on matters of detail.

The precise extent of the work done at this stage, and during the preceding ones, will vary to some extent from project to project, but will include most design details, coordinating the work of all the consultants, including the structural design and building engineering services, and finalising details of the standard of equipment, materials and finishes to be incorporated in the buildings. Any consents relevant to this stage will be applied for.

Discussions will take place, and agreement be reached, as to the tendering procedure for the main contract and sub-contracts, and the advance ordering of any materials critical to achieving the required programme.

If it was not done at the previous stage it will now be necessary to 'freeze' the design, or in other words to refuse to allow any further variations in the design. This is essential because variations which, particularly to the client, may seem of a minor nature can have significant implications on building engineering services, structural design and the construction programme. An example is that the client might decide to exchange an area of office space originally located on the top floor, with a library housing rare books originally located on the ground floor. The client might consider this change was quite insignificant, requiring little more than a change of name, but in fact it is likely to have important implications as regards floor loadings and environmental conditions. As has already been stated it is important that everyone – client and design team – is made aware that any changes at all can result in abortive work, delay and additional costs.

At this stage, as at all other ones, the QS will check that the design is being kept within the cost limits. At the completion of this stage the design team will report back to the client and supply him with copies of relevant drawings and specifications. At this stage the architect is entitled to another 20% of his fees.

10.7. Stage F – Production information

At this stage the detailed drawings and specifications are completed, incorporating the specialist design work done by the consultants and nominated sub-contractors and suppliers. It is an important stage as it involves the preparation of most of the production information which will be used by the contractor to construct the building accurately, economically and efficiently. Particular care therefore needs to be taken at this stage. Failure to do so will inevitably lead to increased costs, either initially because the contractor is not sure what is required and covers the worst possible case when preparing his tender, or at a later stage when missing items form the basis of a claim for extra money.

Coordination is required between the work of the various members of the design team, and meetings will need to take place between the various members to ensure that this happens. A check list may be used to ensure that the production information is properly organised. An example of such a standard check list is shown in Fig. 13.11.

The drawings will include location drawings, such as site layouts and general arrangement drawings. When these are ready, negative copies will be prepared and distributed to the various consultants. This will, for example, enable the building engineering consultant to plot the services on the floor plans. Other drawings to be prepared are assembly drawings and component drawings, and schedules will also be needed.

It is vital to ensure that all drawings are accurate, comprehensive and complete. A drawing check list is a valuable aid in this respect, and a typical example of such a document is given in Fig. 13.12.

Work will be done on the specification. This, in theory, used to be provided by the architect, but increasingly nowadays the quantity surveyor takes responsibility for it, and it becomes an integral part of the BQ.

The production information produced by the architect is also used by the QS to prepare the bills of quantities. The bills are mainly produced at Stage G, but there will often be an overlap between the stages. The architect will need to liaise closely with the QS at Stage F to ensure that the overall cost is kept within the cost limits.

In order to ensure that the work continues to be coordinated, it will be necessary at this stage for all members of the design team to have meetings. The work needs to be planned properly; information from the client and other sources distributed and responsibilities established.

Specialist quotations are likely to be obtained at this stage, and if the proposed programme merits such action, client approval may be obtained to place advance orders for certain materials and work. Applications for any outstanding statutory approvals will have to be made.

This is generally the stage at which preliminary work will take place on tendering and contract arrangements. Agreement needs to be reached with the client as to the names of the contractors who will be invited to tender for the job and a check made as to their suitability.

If consideration is being given to including on the list the names of contractors who are unknown to the architects, they will generally be sent a standard letter asking them to supply information about their organisation and previous jobs they have undertaken. An example of such a letter is shown in Fig. 13.13. Sometimes it will be necessary to obtain references from architects or clients they have previously worked for. An example is shown in Fig. 13.14. Fig. 13.15 shows an assessment form to help decide the suitability of a prospective tenderer.

The tender programme will also have to be decided. Certain information needs to be gathered together in readiness for the preparation of the tender documents. This particularly consists of information which will be included in the 'preliminaries' section of the BQ, such as arrangements for visiting the site, trial/borehole details, site restrictions etc. Often decisions as to the form of contract will also be made at this stage.

Stage F is also an appropriate time to consider, and discuss with the client, the appointment of the clerk of works and resident engineer, assuming that the size of the project warrants such appointments.

10.8 Stage G – Bills of quantities

At this stage the most important thing the architect does is to hand over to the quantity surveyor a full set of his, and the various consultants', drawings, and other documents, so that the bills of quantities can be prepared. This does not mean that every drawing required for the project will necessarily be completed. However it does mean that all drawings, schedules, specification notes, sketches and other information which the quantity surveyor requires in order to prepare accurate bills of quantities must be handed over to him.

The architect's work does not end there however. As the quantity surveyor starts his work there will probably be a steady stream of queries. Some of these will be made and answered by phone. Perhaps the QS will sketch details on A4 paper to record what has been agreed between him and the architect. The architect may also visit the QS's office to resolve some queries. It is also common practice for question and answer sheets to pass to and fro between the architect and QS.

Everyone – for example, the consultants – must be informed of the changes and decisions which have been made because of the day to day discussions between the architect and QS. The architect will of course ensure that his drawings, schedules and other documents are corrected and updated as necessary.

Meetings will need to be held by the design team at this stage. They will include meetings of all team members, and a typical agenda for such a meeting is shown in Fig. 13.16. There will also be less formal meetings between individual members to discuss matters of detail.

As has been previously stated, the BQ is prepared in stages, so initially changes and additions to drawings can be made without too much trouble or inconvenience to the QS and others. However as the time to 'abstract' and 'cast' is reached, and certainly by the time of 'billing', it is too late for any more revisions or additions. This is another stage of the 'freezing' process discussed at Stage E. Changes which are required after this point are too late to be 'billed' and are recorded as 'draft architect's instructions'.

Any work which it is not possible for the QS to detail fully when the work is 'billed', needs to be entered as a prime cost or provisional sum. This will normally include major sub-contracted item, such as building engineering services. This means that before Stage G has ended, it will be essential for the architect to have obtained quotations for all items which will be undertaken by nominated sub-contractors and suppliers.

Stage G is a busy time, particularly for the quantity surveyor, but also for the architect and other members of the design team. In order to ensure that nothing is forgotten, a standard check list for Stage G may be used. An example is shown in Fig. 13.17.

If it has not been done at the previous stage, the architect will have to discuss the appointment of all site staff. In addition to the clerk of works, on a large job with a high building engineering services content, there may also be a specialist clerk of works to take responsibility for this part of the project. There will also be a resident engineer to look after the structural aspects. As the client will pay their salaries and expenses, he will obviously have to agree the terms of their appointment. The people involved in the appointments will probably meet to discuss the matter including the role of each of the site staff. A typical agenda for such a meeting is shown in Fig. 13.18.

The architect will also want to be sure that, as soon as the BQ is complete, the next stage (Stage H – Tender action) can commence. Sets of drawings will therefore be assembled to issue with the BQ and other contract documents, and anything else which needs to be undertaken to proceed to the next stage will be done.

If the final list of tenderers has not already been agreed with the client and quantity surveyor, it should be prepared at this stage. It is common practice at Stage G to send preliminary invitations to all tenderers on the list, in readiness for sending the formal documents when Stage H – Tender action is reached. A typical letter is shown in Fig. 13.19. The progress from inception to tender is a lengthy one, so it is important not to delay this progress by indecision at the point where one stage finishes and another starts.

At this stage, as at all others, it is important that the client is kept fully 'in the picture'. If there is a risk of anything going wrong, the client must be told. For example, it is possible that all approvals have not been received or that the insurance company has not agreed the design and construction. Whatever the possible problem, the client must be informed. In particular, if the decision to proceed before all necessary approvals and agreements has been reached has been at the client's insistence, it must be made quite clear to the client that he is proceeding at his own risk.

Another 20% of the fees are due at this stage, so the architect will present the client with his account for this amount. This is a convenient point to state that the architect must make sure the client pays all outstanding bills. He needs to ensure that bills are submitted and paid promptly.

Having completed his work for this stage, the architect should make sure that his records are kept in order. He will need to file away sets of documents, clearly stamped as follows:

(a) Drawings and documents supplied to the QS.

(b) Drawings and documents supplied to nominated sub-contractors and suppliers.

(c) Architect's draft of instructions to be issued when the contract is let.

(d) Drawings and documents to be supplied as contract documents.

10.9 Stage H – Tender action

At this stage the architect is involved with obtaining tenders and making decisions on the contract. He is in contact with the client and advises on the appointment of the successful contractor.

A meeting with the client is particularly important at this stage, not only to get confirmation to proceed further, but also to settle any outstanding matters in relation to the obtaining of tenders. These could include finalising the choice of contractors who will be invited to tender for the project; agreeing the form of contract, and confirming tender procedures. This will also be a convenient time to check that the client fully understands his own and the architect's roles and responsibilities during the contract period, as well as a further warning of the financial effects of any late changes.

If a preliminary letter to the selected tenderers, confirming their willingness to tender for the job was not sent at the previous stage, it will be done at this stage.

The documents required for tendering will now be assembled into sets, consisting of two copies of the bills of quantities/specification; a set of drawings and schedules, two copies of the form of tender (see typical example in Fig. 13.20); an addressed envelope for the return of the tender; an addressed envelope for the return of one copy of the priced bills; together with a covering letter. (See typical example in Fig. 13.21).

Sometimes a pre-tender meeting will be held with contractors, either collectively or individually. At this meeting the critical aspects of the project will be explained to the contractors, such as the way the job will be organised and controlled; the client's requirements; the programme; the general design and construction, with particular reference to any unusual features, such as special construction techniques and services requirements. The aim should be to draw the attention of the contractors to anything which is not obvious at 'first sight' of the documents, but will have a significant effect on the contractor's costs or programme. It is in everyone's interest that all contractors tender for the job with a full knowledge of the facts. There will be opportunities at such a meeting for the contractors to ask questions.

The letter of invitation to tender can then be issued, together with the documents listed previously. Copies of the letters of invitation to tender will be sent to the client, QS and consultants.

If there are other drawings available, but which were not included in the tender documents, an opportunity will be given for contractors to view them, generally at the architect's office. Sometimes this arrangement will have been mentioned in the bills of quantities, or in the covering letter sent with the tender documents.

At this stage the contractors will also visit the site, and the architect will also have to make any necessary arrangements to facilitate these visits.

It is likely that as the contractors price the work, they will have queries which they will raise with the architect, and which he will answer. It is important that the architect informs all tenderers of any additional information arising from these queries.

Once the tenders have been prepared, arrangements have to be made for their opening. This may be done informally, or at a meeting with, or without, the client. Although at one time it was common for all contractors to be present at the opening of the tenders, this is not now the normal procedure.

A check will need to be made that all documents have been received and are in order. An initial comparison will be made of the tenders, and they may be entered on a standard form, as shown in Fig. 13.23. The lowest tender will then be examined in more detail. If this is in order, this tenderer can expect ultimately to receive the contract. If there are any errors in the tender there are three possible alternatives, as follows:

(a)   The error is corrected, but with an adjustment at the end, so that the contractor stands by his original figure.

(b)   The error is adjusted, but the tender still remains the lowest.

(c)   The tenderer withdraws. In this case the QS will examine the next lowest tender.

Having thoroughly checked the tenders, and made an 'in depth' comparison, the quantity surveyor will report back to the architect, and a tender report, with a recommendation stating which tender should be accepted, will be sent to the client. Depending on the size of the project, this report may be a fairly short letter, or quite a lengthy report which includes a breakdown of the contractors prices.

Once the client has formally accepted the tender, all the tenderers can be notified of the results. Typical letters are shown in Figures 13.24 and 13.25.

Also at this stage, the architect should check there are no outstanding problems – for example, statutory approvals, insurances, rights of way – and advise the client accordingly. He will also check that there are no fees or other costs due from the client.

10.10 Stage J – Project planning

At this stage, the contract documents are prepared and signed. As a preliminary to this, the architect will generally meet with the client, and probably also with the contractor, to clarify and settle any outstanding contractual matters.

At the meeting with the client, if he has not previously done so, the architect needs to explain clearly the detailed working of the contract, particularly the role of the client, as the employer, and the role of the architect, as the employer's agent. It has to be remembered that each of these parties have both responsibilities and rights. It is also important to explain the method of payment, including the use and meaning of interim certificates, architect's instructions, variations and retention. It is particularly important that the client is told tactfully, but firmly, that if the contract is to run smoothly, everyone must understand and honour their rights, responsibilities and limitations. A check list is a useful aid to ensure that nothing is forgotten. An example is shown in Fig. 13.26.

At the meeting with the contractor, the architect will confirm the content of the contact documents, and agree any outstanding contractual points, including the appointment of any nominated sub-contractors. The architect will present the contractor with a list of firms he is considering using, in addition to those already selected, and named at the tender stage. He will check that the contractor has no objection to any of the names on the list. Letters will be sent to both the successful and unsuccessful subcontractors and suppliers. Examples of typical letters are shown in Figures 13.27 and 13.28. Official instructions will also be sent to the contractor telling him to accept the sub-contractor's quotations. The full procedure for placing orders formalising the sub-contract work with the nominated sub-contractors, which was described in Section 8.19 of Chapter 8, will then be set in motion.

The architect will also remind the contractor to obtain his written agreement of the domestic sub-contractors he wishes to use. This is to ensure, for example, that the contractor does not employ a sub-contractor who has recently provided the architect with a poor service on one of his other recent projects.

Critical programme dates will need to be agreed, including dates for the possession of the site. He will probably also inform the contractor of the date of the initial project meeting between the design staff and the contractor. Project meetings are those which take place before work starts on site, at which stage they are termed site meetings.

Following the meeting with the contractor, the contract documents need to be prepared, including the completion of the agreement and appendix, and the deletion of clauses from the conditions as appropriate.

There are a number of operations involved in the signing of the contract, and these are summarised below.

(a) Preparation of sets of contract documents.

(b) Despatch of the contract to the contractor for checking check and signature.

(c) Sending of the contract to the employer for signature.

(d) Checking that all documents are in order.

(e) Sending the contractor a copy of the contract.

(f) Retaining the client's set of the contract documents, with his agreement.

(g) Checking the contractor's insurances.

(h) Informing the client of his insurance responsibilities.

It is now necessary to assemble the production information in readiness for the project meeting. This will consist of two copies of the drawings, schedules, BQ/specification,

as well as any architect's instructions already issued. Copies will also be rec
statutory approvals, any additional decisions on nominated sub-contractors anu
suppliers, and a copy of the architect's and consultant's programmes.

Prior to the project meeting, the architect will often hold a meeting to brief the site supervisory staff. Typical agenda notes for such a meeting are listed below:

(a) Introduction of employer, architectural staff, QS, consultants, COW and RE.

(b) Outline of the main features of the contract as regards the design, construction and programme.

(c) Handing over relevant documents – e.g. copy of contract, drawings, BQ/ specification, drawing register, site diary, report forms, check lists.

(d) Procedures on site instructions, including architect's instructions and COW instructions.

(e) Procedures on communications – e.g. site meetings.

(f) Methods of checking work and maintaining quality control – for example, site tests, conformity with BSSs. and CPs, visits to contractor's and sub-contractor's workshops.

(g) Keeping of site records.

(h) Clarification on limitation of site staff's powers – for example, do nothing which may incur extra costs, or delay the job, without reference to the architect.

One or two project meetings will be necessary before work actually starts on site. Notes on typical agenda items for these meetings are given below:

(a) Introduction of participants, who typically, but not always, will consist of the employer, architect partner, job architect, QS, consultants, COW, RE, contracts manager, and site manager.

(b) Handing over to the contractor of production information previously assembled.

(c) Site arrangements, such as possession date, site access, services diversions, security arrangements, and location of huts, temporary services and sign boards.

(d) Decisions on site meetings, including venue, chairperson, participants, agendas and minutes.

(e) Procedures for communications.

(f) Procedures for issuing instructions and information.

(g) Queries on sub-contractors and suppliers.

(h) Financial arrangements, particularly method of payment, variations and dayworks.

11

Contract procedures generally

11.1 Introduction

The second main part of a building project commences when the work starts on the site, and ends when an analysis is done of the completed building, to decide whether or not the project has been a success. This part is covered by stages K to N of the RIBA Plan of Work.

There are certain key matters which will be considered before the individual stages are discussed. These include site supervision, instructions, variations, dayworks, delays and disputes. All of these items are covered in the JCT Standard Building Contracts.

11.2 Site supervision

Site supervision is achieved by regular site inspections, supported by samples and testing, and formalised by means of site meetings. The purpose of site supervision is to ensure that the contractor constructs the building in accordance with the production information produced by the design team, and within the terms of the contract between the employer and the contractor.

Under the terms of the contract, the contractor has a duty to comply with the specified standards of materials and workmanship, and to keep a competent person on site to take charge of the work. On projects of any significance a site manager will be in overall control, and will have foremen and assistants to help him.

Supervision by the design staff will be divided between the architect and consultants, who will make regular visits to the site, and the clerk of works, and possibly a resident engineer, who will generally be based on site.

As a matter of courtesy the architect should always notify his presence to the site manager when he arrives on site. He must realise that the site manager is in control, and must not give instructions direct to the contractor's workmen. When the architect makes his site inspection he will generally be accompanied by the clerk of works, and possibly by the site manager, or one of his staff.

Architects often use a standard check list for site inspections – see Fig. 13.31. This can be arranged on a trade basis, to make sure everything is properly checked, and in accordance with the production information. A check also needs to be made that the contractor's own supervision is adequate, in respect of matters such as materials and components delivered to the site, including their storage, protection and security, and also in ensuring that the requirements of the Health and Safety at Work Act of 1974 are being met. In addition to keeping a close watch on materials, workmanship and safety, the architect will also expect the contractor to check regularly that the project is on programme.

11.3 Samples and testing

The architect will request samples of various materials and components, such as bricks, tiles, precast concrete units, doors, windows, ironmongery, electrical fittings and sanitary fittings. This is to satisfy him that the architect's and employer's requirements are being met, and also in the case of items showing on the outside of the building, that the requirements of the planning authority are complied with.

In certain cases, for example external facing brickwork, the architect may request that a sample panel of the work be erected. This will be used as a standard for the whole job.

The architect may also make visits to the workshops of the contractor and sub-contractors to ensure that components–e.g. precast concrete panels – are of an acceptable standard and appearance.

Concrete will be regularly tested on site – e.g. by means of a slump test to check workability. The testing of hardened concrete will also take place by sending cubes of concrete to an approved laboratory so their strength can be checked.

Other materials, such as bricks, blocks and floor tiles, may occasionally be sent to the laboratory for testing. In all other cases the architect will expect the standards of the British Standard Specifications and Codes of Practice to be complied with.

11.4 Site meetings

Site meetings are often used to formalise decisions made, and things observed, during the architect's inspections. They are generally divided into two parts, namely (a) policy and (b) production.

Policy meetings

This is likely to be chaired by the architect, working to a standard agenda, and confirming everything discussed, by the issue of minutes. The aim will always be to arrive at clear and unambiguous decisions, and typically there will be a ruling that any dissent must be notified within seven days of receiving the minutes. Typical items on the agenda will be as follows:

(a) Weather report, including working days lost since the previous meeting, due to bad weather conditions.

(b) Labour force on site, by trades.

(c) Programme situation. *NB*: Under the terms of the contract the architect has a right to two copies of the contractor's master programme.

(d) Architect's instructions and variations.

(e) Daywork sheets.

(f) Reports from the contractor, clerk of works, consultants, QS, and sub-contractors.

Production meeting
This is the contractor's meeting, with the purpose of planning and organising the work, and will be chaired by the contractor. The architect or clerk of works will generally attend part or all of the meeting, if requested, and other attenders will consist of key members of the contractor's staff, sub-contractors and suppliers.

11.5 Architect's instructions

However carefully the design team have prepared the production information, almost invariably, there will be a need to issue further instructions, drawings and schedules, after the contract has been signed. These additional detailed requirements and items of information are known as 'architect's instructions'. An example of an architect's instruction is given in Fig. 13.34.

Architects' instructions cover a wide range of items, but they are restricted to matters specifically mentioned in the contract. They include the following:

(a) Compliance with statutory requirements.

(b) Discrepancies in documents.

(c) Levelling and setting out of the works.

(d) Variations.

(e) Making good faults.

(f) Removal of work or materials not in accordance with the contract.

(g) Expenditure of provisional sums.

(h) Sub-contractor's work.

11.6 Variations

Variations are orders, issued during the course of the contract, to alter the originally specified work. They are brought about due to one of the following reasons:

(a) Alterations due to statutory requirements.

(b) Alterations, additions, and omissions, due to either the employer or architect changing their minds.

(c) Errors or omissions in the BQ.

The architect can only issue a variation within the terms of the contract. He cannot issue a variation which would radically change the whole contract – for example, turn an office block into a hospital.

Variation orders generally mean a variation in the amount of the contract. This is achieved either by using prices for a similar items in the BQ, or by using daywork sheets.

A variation is an architect's instruction, but not every architect's instruction is a variation, as some merely amplify previously given information.

11.7 Daywork sheets

When variations are necessary and work is difficult to measure or value – for example, repair work, and forming openings in work already built – there is provision in the JCT Form of Contract to price work through daywork sheets. The daywork sheet will list the following:

(a) Labour, given in hours under the name of individual workmen.

(b) Materials, stating quantity and description.

(c) Plant used.

(d) Transport used.

(e) Overheads, such as insurance and holidays with pay.

(f) Percentage addition, corresponding to the amount in the BQ.

There is a national schedule of daywork rates, issued by the RICS and BEC, which will govern the rates charged.

Daywork sheets must be submitted to the architect or his representative – usually the COW – within a week of the work being carried out. They must relate to an architect's instruction.

The architect or COW will sign the daywork sheet as accurately recording the work carried out. It will be checked by the QS who will satisfy himself that the hours and materials are reasonable for the work undertaken; that the rates are fair, and that the arithmetic is correct.

11.8 Certificates

On most projects the contractor cannot be expected to wait until the end of the job before he is paid. It is usual therefore for him to be paid by instalments, generally every month, so that he is able to finance the work adequately. This is achieved by the architect issuing certificates, indicating to the employer how much money the contractor is entitled to receive.

In deciding the amount of the certificate, the architect is expected to act as an independent professional, and not as the client's agent. In a court case in 1987 (Michael Sallis & Co. Ltd. vs Calil & Calil and William Newman and Associates) the judge ruled as follows. 'It is self evident that a contractor who is party to a JCT contract looks to the architect to act fairly, between him and the building employer in matters such as certificates . . . If the architect unfairly promotes the building employer's interest by low certification, or merely fails to exercise reasonable care and skill in his certification, it is reasonable that the contractor should not only have the right as against the owner to have the certificate reviewed in arbitration, but should also have the right to recover damages as against the unfair architect'.

The certificates issued during the course of the contract are known as 'interim certificates'. When the building is completed, apart from any defects which may come to light during the defects liability period, a 'certificate to practical completion', is issued. When the defects have been made good at the end of the defects liability period, a 'certificate of making good defects' is issued. The final account is then prepared by the quantity surveyor, to calculate what outstanding money is due to the contractor, and the 'final certificate' is issued. Examples of these certificates are shown in Figures 13.35 to 13.38.

Interim certificates are issued at periods stated in the Appendix to the contract, which is usually at monthly intervals. The normal procedure is for the quantity surveyor to make a valuation to decide how much is due to be paid. The amount will consist of the value of completed work, and materials delivered to the site for use on the contract, less previous instalments and the amount deducted for retention.

The retention is the sum of money, expressed as a percentage, which is witheld so as to safeguard the employer in case something goes wrong. All the work has to be completed in a satisfactory manner before the retention money is paid to the contractor. The amount of the retention is written in the appendix to the contract, but generally 5% is retained up to £500,000 and 3% for contracts above this figure.

The contractor in retaining the money is acting as a trustee for the contractor. In other words, although the employer retains the money, it does not belong to him, but is held in trust for the contractor until such times as he has fulfilled all his obligations. This is important if a situation arises where the employer becomes bankrupt, for it means the creditors would not be able to make claims upon the retention money.

When the architect receives the valuation from the quantity surveyor, he issues a certificate to the contractor, except in the case of the local authority edition of the JCT contract, when the certificate is issued direct to the employer.

Under the terms of the contract, the employer is liable to pay the contractor the amount stated in the architect's certificate within 14 days. The architect must, at the time of issuing the certificate, tell the contractor how much of the certificate money is intended for each nominated sub-contractor. There is a special form known as a 'direction' which can be used for this purpose. Each nominated sub-contractor must also be informed.

11.9 Final account

As has been mentioned in Section 11.8 before the architect can issue his final certificate the quantity surveyor prepares a final account.

The final account will be a statement of costs, in which the original contract sum is adjusted by items such as variations, fluctuations in the cost of labour and materials from those prevailing at the time the contract was signed, and accounts from nominated sub-contractors and suppliers.

Any measurement of work necessary for the preparation of the final account will normally be undertaken by the quantity surveyor in conjunction with the contractor. The quantity surveyor has to present his final account to the contractor, and the contract stipulates the period when the final measurement and final account must take place.

Generally both employer and contractor will view the arrival of the final account with considerable interest. The employer will desire to be told of his total commitment, and the contractor will be anxious to receive the remainder of the money which is due to him.

11.10 Delays

It is an unfortunate fact of 'building life' that building projects often run behind programme, and are not completed by the date stated in the contract. These delays may be the fault of the contractor, the employer, the design team, or sometimes of outside circumstances for which nobody is really responsible.

The contract includes an agreed date when all work will be completed. Also within the contract is a provision under which the contractor can claim for 'an extension of time'. The circumstances under which the contractor may claim for an extension are given under Section 11.11 below.

The contractor must give the architect written notification of any delay, and the involvement of any nominated sub-contractors. The effect of the delay must be stated, so that a revised completion date can be fixed.

If the delay is due to the inefficiency or incompetence of the contractor, and this results in the contractor failing to complete the building by the date stated in the contract, the contractor is liable to pay the employer what is known as 'liquidated and ascertained damages'. The amount of these damages are stated in the Appendix to the contract, and is usually fixed at so much money per day or week.

11.11 Extension of time

An extension of time can be granted to the contractor if delay is due to the following:

Action of the architect or employer

(a) Variations.

(b) Architect's instructions which delay work.

(c) Late issue of drawings etc.

(d) Delay by employer's directly employed staff affecting work – e.g. an artist.

(e) Opening up of completed work later found to be correct.

Action outside the control of parties to the contract

(a) Force majeure – eventualities not specifically mentioned elsewhere in the contract.

(b) Exceptionally inclement weather.

(c) Fire, flood, storm etc.

(d) Civil commotion.

In a similar way to that previously mentioned under Section 11.8 – Certificates, the architect is also expected to act as an independent professional in the matter of granting an extension of time. He will be aware of the fact that, if he certifies an extension of time which is too short, the contractor may suffer a loss, while if the period is too long the client will be the one to suffer. In the court case previously mentioned under Section 11.8, one of the claims made by the contractor was that the architect was in breach of a duty of care in authorising an extension to the contract period, both in respect of the length of extension given, and also failure to grant an extension with reasonable speed.

11.12 Death of architect

If an architect dies during the course of a contract, the employer will have to reach agreement with the contractor regarding the appointment of another architect. If necessary the matter will have to be referred to arbitration – see Section 11.16 of this chapter. The matter cannot be dealt with by the deceased person's (i.e. the architect's) executors, because the architect's appointment is a personal contract between the architect and his client.

11.13 Death of employer

The situation is considered to be different if the employer (client) dies. In this case the employer's executors are expected to take over the role of employer, and discharge his responsibilities and liabilities under the terms of the contract.

11.14 Bankruptcy

If during the course of the contract the contractor becomes bankrupt, the employer is entitled to employ another contractor to complete the building work.

In the words of the JCT Form of Contract 'the employment of the contractor under the contract is automatically determined' – i.e. brought to an end.

It is generally assumed that any materials on the building site are the property of the employer. The onus is on the trustees in bankruptcy to prove otherwise.

11.15 Disputes

The JCT and other forms of contract have been prepared with great care, and should cover most eventualities. Many disputes which arise will be settled amicably by the parties involved, and the architect will have a special role to play in this respect.

Although it is the client who employs him and pays his fees, he has a responsibility to ensure that both the employer (client) and the contractor are fairly treated under the terms of the contract. The architect is expected to act impartially in this respect, and in effect becomes an arbitrator – a person who settles disputes.

In cases which cannot be settled by the parties to the contract, even with the honest efforts of the architect, the contract contains a provision for the matter to be referred to arbitration. The alternative to this is for the party who considers he is being unfairly treated to bring a lawsuit against the other party. It is best to try and avoid such a situation, for litigation is invariably a longer and more expensive method of settling disputes than arbitration.

Arbitration is particularly appropriate when the dispute is technical rather than legal. It has the further advantage that the parties involved in the dispute have some control over the choice of arbitrator, but no control over the choice of judge if the matter is referred to a court.

11.16 Arbitration

Arbitration means to settle a dispute between two or more parties by appointing a person, called an arbitrator, to whom both parties have agreed to submit their differences, and be bound by his decision.

If the parties cannot agree upon the choice of an arbitrator, a suitable person will be selected by the President or Vice-President of the RIBA.

Generally the person appointed as arbitrator will be either an architect or surveyor with a thorough knowledge of arbitration procedures, or a lawyer with some knowledge of building. His fees are paid jointly by the parties to the dispute.

Matters which can be referred to arbitration during the progress of the work are given in the JCT standard contracts. They are:

(a) Appointment of a new architect or quantity surveyor. For example, where the previous architect or quantity surveyor has died.

(b) Validity of an architect's instruction.

(c) Witholding or incorrect preparation of certificates.

(d) Dispute in connection with the employment by the employer of others to carry out the work when the contractor has failed to comply with the architect's instructions.

(e) Dispute in connection with an extension of time.

(f) Result of outbreak of war.

Other matters can generally be dealt with by arbitration after the practical completion of the contract.

In 1988 the Joint Contracts Tribunal published its Arbitration Rules, which lays down standard procedures for every instance where the parties to a building contract are referred to arbitration. The Rules allow for the following arbitration arrangements:

A document of arbitration

With this method the claimant has to serve his statement, in writing, within 14 days after a preliminary meeting. The respondent has to serve a written statement giving his defence within a further 14 days. The claimant then has the right to serve a reply to the respondent's defence within a further 14 days.

The arbitrator may decide to interview the parties to receive further clarification of the documents. The arbitrator has to publish his decision within 28 days of receiving the last statement. There is provision in this method for the respondent to serve a counter claim with his defence, and the other party will also be given a 14 days period to reply to the counter claim.

A full procedure with an oral hearing

The first part of the arbitration is concerned with the exchange of written statements, and follows a similar pattern to the method referred to under 'A document of arbitration'. The arbitrator then arranges the place, date and time of the oral hearing, when both parties will present their case. The arbitrator has to publish his decision within 28 days of the oral hearing.

A short procedure with an oral hearing

This method can only be adopted with the agreement of both parties to the dispute. The oral hearing takes place within 21 days of a preliminary meeting. The parties must send to the arbitrator, and to each other, at least seven days before the oral hearing, copies of the documents which will be used at the hearing. The arbitrator must give his decision within seven days of the hearing.

11.17 Site diary

This will be kept by the COW on a daily basis to record anything of importance which happens on the site, including the following:

(a) Time lost by bad weather.

(b) Visitors to site.

(c) Deliveries of materials.

(d) Start of key areas of work.

(e) Arrival of sub-contractors.

(f) Information requested by contractor.

(g) Comments made to contractor, particularly about faulty work.

(h) Discrepancies between work carried out and drawings, for whatever reasons.

(i) Results of site tests.

11.18 Weekly reports

These are often prepared on a standard form (see Fig. 13.32) by the COW, and sent to the architect. Information given will commonly consist of the following:

(a) Workmen on site, by trades.

(b) Stoppages, in hours.

(c) Delays with reasons.

(d) Plant and materials on site.

(e) Plant and materials shortages.

(f) Drawings and information received.

(g) Drawings and information given.

(h) Visitors to site.

11.19 Recording progress

One of the requirements of the JCT Standard Forms of Building Contracts is that the contractor provides the architect with two copies of his master programme for undertaking the work. If the architect has agreed to a revised completion date for the contract, the contractor is also obliged to supply the architect with updated copies of the programme.

The programme is not a contractual document, and the manner in which the contractor undertakes the work is generally at his discretion. However, the contractor's programme will generally provide a useful guide against which the architect can measure the progress of the construction work.

Once work commences on site, regular meetings will be held (see Fig. 13.33 for typical agenda) and one of the most important function of these meetings is to monitor progress. If any change to the original completion date is envisaged, this will generally be recorded in the minutes of the meeting. Progress will also be recorded in the COW's weekly reports (see Fig. 13.32).

The COW's site diary which is kept by the clerk of works on daily basis, is useful in immediately drawing attention to occurrences which can have an effect on the construction programme. Progress photographs also have a useful part to play, and these must obviously be dated so as to provide a pictorial record of progress at particular dates.

11.20 Recording site happenings

The minutes of site meetings, the COW's site diary and weekly reports, and the progress photographs will also be a means of recording all other items which can influence the progress, cost and standard of the construction work.

This information is invaluable if disputes arise, particularly if they result in claims by the contractor for extra money or an extension of time. People's memories are sometimes inaccurate, and written evidence is generally necessary to settle disputes.

All the architect's instructions must be in writing, and a careful record must be kept as to the dates specific drawings were supplied to the contractor and sub-contractors, including the revision letters.

11.21 Information to be provided by the contractor

The JCT Standard Forms of Building Contracts places the contractor under an obligation to provide the architect with certain information during the course of the contract. This is summarised as follows.

(a) Provision and updating of master programme.

(b) Return of drawings to architects if requested.

(c) Proof, if requested, that materials used comply with the architect's specification.

(d) Notice of any delays.

(e) Information on claims by nominated sub-contractors.

(f) Documents necessary to adjust the contract sum.

(g) Notice of fluctuations in the cost of labour and materials from the figures originally entered in the BQ.

11.22 Insurances

The architect has the responsibility of ensuring that work on the site does not begin until the contractor has taken out the insurances necessary to cover any eventuality likely to occur.

The JCT Standard Forms of Contract requires the contractor to arrange for the following insurances.

(a) Insurances against injury to persons and property due to the negligence of the contractor, or those he is responsible for. This will generally be covered by the contractor's own comprehensive policy, and the architect will need to check that the cover in this policy is adequate, and that the premiums have been paid. The Appendix to the Conditions of Contract states the amount of cover required.

(b) Joint insurance, in the names of the employer and the contractor, against claims for loss or damage to any property, which is not due to the contractor's negligence. This insurance is covered by a provisional sum in the bills of quantities. Before the work commences on site, the architect gives an instruction to the contractor on how this provisional sum is to be spent. Although this insurance is taken out in the joint names of the employer and contractor, it is the responsibility of the contractor to arrange the insurance, and pay the premiums. The architect will however check that the cover is adequate, and the premiums have been paid.

(c) Insurance of the works against fire and other risks. Responsibility for this risk may vary from contract to contract, between the employer and contractor. It is important for the architect to check the responsibilities of these two parties, so that sufficient cover has been arranged, and that the premiums have been paid. The situation tends to become particularly complicated when the building work consists of extensions and alterations to existing buildings.

Ensuring that the right kind of insurance cover has been arranged for all likely eventualities can be a difficult business, and the architect needs to discuss the matter with his client, and if necessary with the contractor, and an insurance broker or other expert, before the building work commences.

This is borne out by a case (Gold vs Patman and Fotherington) which came before the courts in 1958. In this case the employer sued the contractor for failing to insure him against the risk of damage to properties adjoining the building site being likely to collapse or subside. During the erection of an office block on the employer's site, piling operations took place and resulted in damage to adjoining properties, and the employer was sued by the adjoining owner. In turn, the employer sued the contractor. The employer lost his case against the contractor on the grounds that the obligation imposed by the bills of quantities was for the contractor to insure himself and not the employer.

12

Contract stages

12.1 Introduction

This chapter deals with the three stages included in the RIBA Plan of Work which takes place after the contract has been signed. They are:

Stage K   Operations on site.
Stage L   Completion.
Stage M   Feedback.

12.2 Stage K – operations on site

At this stage the site is handed over to the contractor, and the actual building process commences. Throughout this period, regular site meetings are held, and the architect, with the help of other members of the design team, will carry out overall supervision, and arrange for payment of the work.

From the point when the site is handed over to the contractor, until the finished building is handed over to the client, the site becomes the total responsibility of the contractor. In handing over the site, the architect should remind the contractor of his obligations in respect of security and safety. The contractor should be informed of any special conditions applying to the site, such as rights of way, preservation of existing trees, and protection of neighbouring properties. The handing over of the site should normally be done by means of a letter sent by the architect to the contractor, which records both the date and the conditions which apply to the site. A typical letter is shown in Fig. 13.29.

Now that the work is about to start on site, the architect will check that the contractor has copies of all the drawings and other information he requires, including the full details for setting out. He will remind the contractor of the importance of keeping one set of contract drawings and one copy of the bills of quantities on the site.

Generally the contractor and architect will meet on site to resolve all outstanding items relating to the setting out of the work which were not settled at the project meeting held during the previous stage. These could include some of the following:

(a) Siting of temporary huts, storage areas, mixing areas, temporary roads and pavings, and spoil heaps.

(b) Position of fences, hoardings, and access into the site.

(c) Position of the main sign board, to the architect's design.

(d) Protection to existing property, trees etc.

(e) Position of site datum and bench marks.

(f) Problems relating to setting out.

If necessary, the architect will check the setting out and levels, or authorise the clerk of works or resident engineer to do so on his behalf.

During the whole period that building operations are taking place on the site, the architect has responsibility for general supervision. Regular inspections will take place, and liaison will be maintained with the clerk of works, resident engineer and the consultants, to ensure that specified materials and constructional techniques are employed, and that adequate quality control is maintained. A Site Inspection Check List is a useful aid to ensure that the inspection and supervision is carried out in a methodical and thorough way. Typical check lists are shown in Figures 13.30 and 13.31.

The clerk of works will be carrying out a continuous check to ensure that all work is undertaken in accordance with the latest drawings and specifications, and will inform the architect immediately he notices any discrepancies. He will issue a weekly report to the architect summarising the current situation on the site. A typical example of such a report is shown in Fig. 13.32.

It is important that records and reports, including the COW's daily site diary, are kept up to date. Progress photographs should be taken, generally in conjunction with the contractor. All drawings must be updated, particularly where they relate to items which will be 'hidden' on completion of the work – For example, the precise position of the underground drains. On most projects, changes, even if they are of a very minor nature, take place during the course of site operations. It is important that such changes are noted, and a full set of record drawings maintained.

Architects' instructions and variations will be issued as necessary, and both the client and quantity surveyor will be kept informed. All instructions should be issued to the contractor, including those for sub-contractors and suppliers. Oral instructions should be confirmed in writing within seven days, and the clerk of works instructions within two days. Written confirmation of architect's instructions will generally be achieved by use of standard forms. A typical example is shown in Fig. 13.34.

If there are still sub-contractors or suppliers who have not been nominated, the architect will have to do so sufficiently early so as not to prejudice the contractor's agreed programme. Instructions will be issued to the contractor, and the unsuccessful sub-contractors and suppliers will be notified.

Particular attention will be paid to any circumstances which could lead to delays. Preventive action will be taken where possible, but if delays are unavoidable it is necessary to establish who is responsible, as there are contractual obligations. All claims for an extension of time will be considered, and the architect will issue a Notification of an Extension of Time where applicable, generally by issue of a standard form.

Interim certificates, based on the QS's valuation, will be issued at regular intervals, generally every month, and dayworks will be authorised as necessary. The architect, under the guidance of the QS, will direct the contractor as to the amount included in an interim certificate for each sub-contractor, and will also inform the sub-contractor of this fact, generally by means of a standard form. The contractor has the right to expect that the certificates, including those for nominated sub-contractors, will be issued by the architect strictly in accordance with the terms of the contract, and the architect has a responsibility to ensure that this happens. Standard forms will generally be used for certificates, and a typical form is shown in Fig. 13.35.

The architect will hold regular meetings at the site, generally every month, although on some contracts they may take place more frequently. These meetings will be attended by the design staff, including the clerk of works and resident engineer, the contractor, and also by sub-contractors and suppliers as and when required. It is important to insist that everyone attending has the power to act for their respective companies, so that firm decisions can be made at the meetings. It is also important that the minutes are circulated soon after the meeting – within 24 hours is a reasonable period – and that the minutes clearly state what action is required, and by whom. Agreement should be reached with those attending the meetings that any disagreements with the recorded minutes must be notified to the architect within seven days of receiving the minutes. A typical agenda for an architect's site meeting is shown in Fig. 13.33.

The contractor will normally hold his own production meeting prior to the architect's progress meeting. This will be arranged and chaired by the contractor, but the architect will be expected to attend if invited to do so by the contractor.

Contact must also be kept with all members of the design team regarding matters of design. On large projects there will probably be regular meetings, but on smaller projects the contact may be more informal. The main aim is to ensure that everyone is fully aware of their responsibilities, and knows precisely 'who is supposed to do what – and when'. Particular care needs to be taken to ensure that all drawings and other information required by the contractor are available to suit his agreed programme.

Regular contact will be maintained with the client. He will be particularly concerned with anything relating to progress, costs, and the finished building. The client should be sent copies of the minutes of site meetings, even if he does not attend them. He should also be sent a financial statement each month with the total cost forecast. Care should be taken to ensure that the client's approval is received for any additional costs arising from changes in the design, additional items of work, and adjustments to the provisional sums.

As this stage draws to a close, it is necessary for the architect to prepare for completion. He will need to collect 'as built' record drawings together with all the information needed for the Building Owner's Manual.

It will also be necessary to initiate action for the commissioning and testing of the services installation. The procedure for this will have to be agreed with the other parties who are involved, but typically will be as follows:

(a) Agree programme.

(b) Sub-contractors test their services.

(c) Consultants then supervise tests.

(d) Systems charged with water, air etc.

(e) Systems regulated and balanced.

12.3 Stage L – completion

The main event at this stage is to accept the building on behalf of the client. There is also work to be done in preparing for the Handover, and matters to be settled after the Handover has taken place.

The first activity is a Pre-Completion Check which consists of the following items:

(a) Instruct the contractor to give adequate notice of practical completion and check, with the aid of the COW, that the date given by the contractor is realistic. NB: Practical Completion is the stage when:
   (i) All work has been completed in accordance with the contract documents and the architect's instructions.
   (ii) The building is ready for the client – i.e. he can take it over for its proper use.

(b) Inform the client of the proposed handover date and explain the procedure for this stage, including the need to insure the building and contents prior to handover.

(c) Inspect the building, listing the outstanding work – this is commonly known as the 'snagging list' – and circulate the list.

(d) Ensure that services installations are tested and commissioned as agreed at the end of Stage K – operations on site.

(e) Make sure that 'as built' record drawings are up to date and ready for issue. Two copies will be supplied – generally one to the client and one to a third party, e.g. the client's bank. These record drawings will generally include the architect's, consultant's and sub-contractor's drawings.

(f) Make sure that the Building Owner's Manual, particularly the section dealing with services items, is ready.

When the pre-completion checks have taken place, the Handover Meeting can be held. The programme for this meeting will generally include the following:

(a) An explanation by the architect as to the purpose of the meeting.

(b) A tour of the building during which:
   (i) Defects are noted and listed.
   (ii) A check is made that the contractor's property has been, or will be removed, from the site.
   (iii) A check is made that the services are working, meters are read, and fuel stocks are checked.

(c) The handover takes place, including the following:
   (i) A set of record drawings.
   (ii) Building owner's Manuals, which includes information on operating the services and on maintenance.
   (iii) Keys.

(d) The procedure for the Defects Liability Period is agreed.

Following the Handover, the Certificate of Practical Completion can be issued. An example is shown in Fig. 13.36. The architect issues this to the contractor, with copies to the client and quantity surveyor.

At this stage:

(a)   The contractor is entitled to receive part of the Retention Fund.

(b)   The Defects Liability Period begins.

(c)   The contractor is no longer responsible for insuring the work.

(d)   The period of final measurement begins.

(e)   Any outstanding matters in dispute can be referred to arbitration as they occur. For example, a dispute on an architect's instruction, or improper witholding of money – but most items will await completion of the contract.

The employer (client) now takes full responsibility for the building and the contractor, consultants and sub-contractors explain the workings of the equipment to the employer's staff.

Once the employer takes over the building, the Defects Liability Period commences. This is the period of time, generally six months, when any defects due to faulty workmanship have to be put right by the contractor.

The role of the architect in respect of the Defects Liability Period can be summarised as follows:

(a)   The architect, after Practical Completion, makes sure the contractor has a full list of defects apparent at that stage.

(b)   He checks that the contractor is carrying out the work in accordance with an agreed programme.

(c)   If necessary, he visits the site to supervise the work.

(d)   He asks the client to tell him of any defects which occur during the Defects Liabilty Period. These defects may be dealt with immediately, or later.

(e)   About three or four weeks before the end of the Defects Liability Period, the architect visits the site, to meet the client, and prepare a list of defects. This is generally done with the COW, but sometimes the COW will undertake this task on his own.

(f)   He sends the list of outstanding defects to the contractor.

(g)   He agrees a programme of work.

After the end of the Defects Liabilty Period the architect has to:

(a)   Check with the contractor that all outstanding work has been completed.

(b)   Make arrangements for the final inspection.

(c)   Make the final inspection, with the client and the contractor, and probably with the COW, QS, and consultants also in attendance.

Following the final inspection, the Certificate of Making Good Defects is issued to the contractor. An example is given in Fig. 13.37. This signifies the completion of the job, and means that the second half of the Retention Fund is released to the contractor.

The QS now prepares his Final Account, sending a copy to the contractor, and issues the Final Certificate. An example is given in Fig. 13.38. All fee accounts should by now be settled, including the 25% of the architect's fee not paid during the pre-contract stage.

12.4 Stage M – feedback

The architect has the following two responsibilities after the building is completed.

A continuing liability in the case of building failure
The architect and the contractor have a legal responsibility if there is a failure in the building. This was discussed in Chapter 4.

A voluntary responsibility to benefit from lessons learnt
In order to benefit from the results of a project, the architect can ask himself a series of pertinent questions. Some examples are given below:

(a) Was the job profitable as far as the design team were concerned? If not – why?

(b) Did the design process work smoothly?

(c) Did the contractor work well?

(d) Was there a good working relationship between the design staff and the contractor's staff?

(e) Could the design staff, by different detailing etc., have helped the contractor erect a better building, more quickly?

(f) Does the completed building look nice, and fit in with its surroundings?

(g) Are there any details which were particularly successful, or unsuccessful?

(h) Does the building function properly?

(i) What does the client think of the building?

13

Standard documentation

13.1 Introduction

If a building project is to progress smoothly and to programme, it is vital that everyone involved knows exactly what they have to do, and when and how it has to be done. The architect has a special responsibility for much of the documentation for this decision-making process. In practice it involves use of written material such as letters, forms, check lists and agendas of meetings.

This chapter includes some examples of these types of documentation. They all relate to the factory and office block project mentioned previously.

13.2 Letters

Traditionally, letters are either individually composed, or are produced in a standard format, sometimes with blank spaces for filling in for specific situations. In more recent years the advent of word processing has meant that a standard letter format can be adapted to give the impression that the letter was individually produced for a particular project. The letters included in this chapter can be assumed to be mainly of this type.

13.3 Forms

Standard forms giving information and instructions are widely used for building projects. Some are produced by individual practices, and others by professional bodies such as the RIBA and BIAT. Examples of both of these types are included in this chapter. The RIBA forms are included by kind permission of RIBA Publications Ltd., from whom copies can be obtained.

13.4 Check lists

Some architectural practices make use of standard check lists to remind their staff of the many tasks which have to be done during the course of a building project. These check lists are of particular value to less experienced architects and technicians, but they can help even the most experienced staff to achieve a systematic approach to their work.

13.5 Agendas

Agendas can be considered as a form of check list. They consist of a list of items which need to be considered at a meeting, and help to ensure that nothing is forgotten. After the meeting, a summary of what took place is produced as the minutes of the meeting.

Lane & Ralph △ *Architects*

BRIEFING CHECKLIST

PART 1 INFORMATION FROM CLIENT

Generally

1.01 Client's Name. *Mr. A. Henry – Managing Director*
      Address. *Henry Electronics Ltd.*
      100 Hart Road, London, SW1

      Telephone No.

1.02 Date and Place of Briefing Meeting. *1st March 1989. Client's office*

1.03 People present. *Mr. A. Henry, Mr. A. Lane*

1.04 Client's representative *Mr. A Henry or in his absence*
      for future queries. *Mr. F. McCarthy Works Manager*

1.05 Type of project. *Factory with office block*

1.06 List any drawings *Un-numbered plan of site copied from*
      available from client. *conveyance*

1.07 Names and addresses of
      any other architects/ *none*
      professionals involved.

1.08 Client's initial *Buildings completed and occupied*
      programme requirements. *by client September 1990*

1.09 Client's Target Cost. *£1,000,000*

1.10 Any other relevant information available from
      client.

Approvals at Present Stage

1.11 Has Outline Planning Permission been granted? *no*

      If so, obtain copy or details.

1.12 Has any Local Authority, Government Department,
      or other authority made any comments on the
      proposed development? *no*

      If so obtain details.

1.13 Are any activities required in the building for
      which licences might be required? E.g. Public
      Assembly, Music and Dancing, Liquor.
      no

Site

1.14 If site has not been purchased, what location and plan area is client considering?

1.15 If site has been obtained, state :

Location of site. *Stephen's Industrial Estate, Box Hill, Epsom*

Position of site related to O.S. plan or deed plan etc. *no*

Is client freeholder or leaseholder of site? *Freeholder, but check with solicitor*

Is any part of the site agriculturally let? *no*

If so, give names and addresses of agricultural tenants.

1.16 Any known easements or rights affecting development of site. *check with solicitor*

1.17 Existing buildings to be retained or demolished. *small building to north west of site can be demolished*

1.18 Existing External Works to be retained or demolished.

1.19 Existing Natural Features to be retained or demolished. *Keep mature trees if possible*

1.20 Can client give any information on:

Levels? *mainly flat with knolls around perimeter*

Nature of soil? *probably clay*

Bearing pressure? *not known*

Water table? *no water problems known*

Underground workings, faults, restrictions? *none known*

1.21 Does client know of any private sewers, septic tanks, watercourses, water supply etc., available for this development?

no

1.22 Does client have knowledge of public services available?

Soil sewer.

Surface water sewer.

Water supply.

} *Mr. Henry believes they are all available around site perimeter*

Gas supply.

Electricity supply.

Telephone.

} *Mr. Henry believes these are available*

1.23 Names and addresses of adjoining owners, if known to client.

not known

Preferences

1.24 For any materials, externally and internally.

likes brick

1.25 For any structural system or construction.

wide spans in factory area

1.26 For any roof type (e.g. flat or pitched.)

dislikes flat roof

1.27 For any particular standards and methods or air conditioning, ventilation, heating, lighting.

air conditioning for clean room area

1.28 How important is freedom from maintenance?

very important

Internal Planning and Constr

1.29 Determine and schedule _____ required, with reference to the following where _____

(a) Activity; floor area _____ _____ location
    (basement, ground or u _____ _____ber of occupants
    and sex.

general production a _____ *350 sq.m. ground floor*
'clean room' area _____ *50 " " " "*
warehouse _____ *0 " " "*
office _____ *ground or first floor*

(b) Circulation spaces. *leave to architect*

(c) Any limits to clear heights, spans and openings.
In factory area 4·5m clear ht. throughout and maximum spans

(d) Any special construction of finishes required.
'clean finish' very important

(e) Floor loading.

(f) Special Fixtures e.g. lifts, cranes, conveyors, machine
bases, ducts, pits and tanks.
conversions required

(g) Structural provision for future installations or openings.
facilities for extension

(h) Special Conditions e.g. fumes, dust, noise, vibration, waste
disposal, trade effluents, fire protection, mechanical
handling, security.
discuss with Mr. McCarthy

1.30 Determine Amenities e.g. toilets, washrooms, showers, lockers,
changing rooms, rest rooms, first aid, canteen, recreation rooms,
kitchen, tea points, cleaners store, refuse disposal.
all above areas, except for recreation room, required

1.31 Any anticipated provision for :
Water storage
Gas meter
Transformers, main switches, distribution switches
Boilers, fuel storage
Ventilation plant, including cooling towers
Lightning protection
Aerials
} architects/ consultants to decide

External Planning and Construction

1.32 Site coverage.   *?*

1.33 New Accesses from adjoining highways.   *yes*

1.34 Planting.   *Landscaped site preferred*

1.35 Car Parking - staff and visitors.   *Mr. McCarthy to provide information*

1.36 External Materials, including signs. *architects to decide*

1.37 New Service Roads - type, widths, loads. *required*
                                                Mr. McCarthy will
1.38 Gross circulation area. ←———— *provide details*

1.39 Service Vehicles :

    Uncovered parking *required. Area to be supplied later*

    Garaging *not required*

    Maintenance provision " "

    Loading dock " "

    Turn around space *required*

    Petrol storage and pumps *not required*

1.40 Cycle storage. *to consider and give architect's decision*

1.41 Security :

    Fencing *yes*

    Gates *yes*

    Gate control *yes*

    Weighbridge *no*

1.42 Any special external services requirements e.g. flooding.
    no

1.43 Any future extensions to be provided for.
    yes to both factory, warehouse and office block

Fig. 13.1 Briefing check list (obtained from client)

Lane & Ralph △ *Architects*

Tel: 01-394 12340
Our ref:
Your ref:

Hogsmill House,
Sarah's Drive,
Stoneleigh,
Surrey.

1st March 1989

Mr A Henry
Henry Electronics Ltd.
100 Hart Road
London
SW1

Dear Mr Henry,

PROPOSED FACTORY AND OFFICE BLOCK, STEPHEN'S INDUSTRIAL ESTATE, BOX HILL

Further to our meeting this morning we are pleased to accept your
invitation to act as architects for the above project. I enclose a copy
of the Briefing Check List which I completed at the meeting; these
provide an outline brief of your requirements.

Our services will consist of the design of the buildings and external
works items; the preparation of production information; obtaining all
necessary statutory approvals; advice on the appointment of a
contractor; inspection of the construction work on site; and the issue
of architect's certificates authorizing payment in monthly stages to the
contractor. As agreed our fees will be 5% of the final contract sum
payable in instalments, as described in the R.I.B.A. Conditions of
Engagement. A marked copy of this document is enclosed for your
information. The 5% fee does not include V.A.T. which is chargeable at
15% on our fees, or other disbursements and out of pocket expenses.

We also confirm your agreement to the appointment of the following
specialist consultants.

a) Quantity Surveyors. Vincent, John and Partners.
   To prepare Bills of Quantities, and financial advice and supervision
   throughout the pre-contract and contract period.

b) Structural Engineers. Lewis and Son.
   To prepare the design, and production information for the structural
   work, and inspection of this work on site.

c) Building Services Engineer. John Andrew MCIBS.
   To prepare the design, and production information for heating, air
   conditioning, ventilation, plumbing, drainage and electrical services
   and inspection of this work on site.

Consultants fees should not exceed 6% of the final contract sum.

As mentioned at our meeting we would appreciate it if you would check the following matters with your legal advisors.
a) Confirmation that you have freehold ownership of the site.
b) Detail any restrictions on the land e.g. rights of way, restrictive covenants, easements.
c) Supply a plan defining the precise boundaries of the site.
d) Details of any previous planning permission given for the site.

We will shortly send you a Memorandum of Agreement to formalize the contract between us. Meanwhile we are commencing work on our Feasibility Report.

We would like to thank you for choosing our practice to undertake this project for you. Every effort will be made to provide you with a building which meets all your requirements, within your required time scale.

If you have any queries please do not hesitate to contact me.

Yours sincerely,

A Lane

Arnold Lane

Fig. 13.2 Typical letter sent to client after initial meeting

Lane & Ralph △ *Architects*

<u>DETAILED BRIEFING AT STAGE B - FEASIBILITY</u>

ROOM / AREA NAME   clean room

FUNCTION OF ROOM / AREA   assembly of electronic components

SHAPE / PLAN SIZE / HEIGHT   350 square metres floor area
4.5 metres clear height

ROLE OF PEOPLE USING ROOM / AREA AND NO. OF OCCUPANTS
assembly workers   35 persons

SPATIAL RELATIONSHIPS   between general production area and
warehouse entered via special
air conditioned lobby as Hart Road
factory — take details from factory.

SPECIAL FEATURES, INCLUDING LAYOUT, CLEAR SPAN
squarish shape required. maximum clear span.
generally copy arrangement at Hart Road factory

WALL FINISHES   FLOOR FINISHES   CEILING FINISHES
smooth, clean   perforated   perforated illuminated
surfaces   computer type   ceiling
floor

DOOR REQUIREMENTS
smooth finish, heavy duty, self closing

FIXTURES
as list supplied by Mr. McCarthy

NATURAL LIGHTING REQUIREMENTS
750 lux

HEATING   kept to constant 20°c

AIR CONDITIONING   yes, downward flow of conditioned air
from perforated ceiling to perforated floor

VENTILATION

Fig. 13.3 Part of detailed briefing (obtained from client)

Lane & Ralph △ *Architects*

BRIEFING CHECK LIST

<u>PART 2 INFORMATION FROM INITIAL SITE INSPECTION</u> 24th March 1989

2.01 Notes on Buildings and External works to be demolished or retained
e.g. size, construction and condition.

brick building 4 x 4 m. to north west of site about
24 metres from south west boundary

2.02 Impression of contours

fairly flat and level but with knolls very close
to the perimeter of site at the north east,
north west and south west boundary

2.03 Notes on existing natural features including views, existing
trees.

mature oak tree near the centre of site must be
retained, if possible also retain group of trees
in west corner of site

2.04 Notes on adjoining buildings :

Owners / occupiers Pound Products Ltd to south east
boundary

Height about 7 metres

Construction, materials, condition

plastic coated sheeting, flat roof — see sketch attached
buildings are about 10 years old.

Obvious rights enjoyed right of support

Proximity to site close to south east boundary

2.05 Other information. Take photographs, preliminary sketches,
measurements if necessary and feasible.

photographs and sketches attached
public right of way exists along north west
boundary

Fig. 13.4 Information from site inspection

Lane & Ralph △ *Architects*

SITE AND BUILDING SURVEY CHECK LIST

SITE SURVEY

Overall measurements of site.
Measurements relating buildings to site.
Triangulation of site.
Levels of site and ground levels of buildings, and relate to suitable datum.
Heights, thicknesses and materials of boundaries.
Heights, rights of light and general description of adjacent buildings.
General description of existing buildings on site.
Fences, railings.
Gates.
Steps, ramps.
Paths.
Paved areas.
Roads, drives.
Landscaping and natural features.
Good and bad views.
Type of soil.
Availability of gas services, with any evidence of location.
Availability of electricity services with details of any overhead lines.
Availability of telephone services with details of any overhead lines.
Availability of water services, with any evidence of location.
Drainage including surface water, soil and waste, gulleys, ventilation pipes, fresh air inlets, manholes (size and depth) direction and flow.

BUILDING SURVEY

Floor Plans

Overall measurements of the building.
Running measurements in each room picking up door and window openings etc., measured to brick jambs.
Floor to ceiling heights.
Through measurements wherever possible.
Diagonal measurements.
Construction joints.
Thickness and construction of all walls.
Particulars and position of columns.
Direction of floor joists and positions of beams and roof beams.
Particulars and positions of roof lights.
Materials and finishes to walls, floors and ceilings.
Sanitary fittings.
Particulars and sizes of doors and fanlights.
Heights from floor to sill and to head of all windows.
Roof space access.
Stairs and changes of levels.
Ventilators and louvres.
Trim (architraves, skirtings, window boards)
Drainage to show all internal soil and rainwater disposal pipes, ventilation pipes, internal gulleys, manholes (size and depth) and direction of flow.

Water supply and other plumbing, including stopcocks, piping runs, insulation, cisterns (sizes and means of support).
Hot water systems, including heater, piping runs, h.w cylinder, expansion tank.
Heating system, including boiler, plant items, fittings.
Fuel storage.
Electrical installation including external wiring, point of entry, meter, lighting and socket outlets, switches, fittings and equipment.
Gas installation including meter, piping, points, fittings and equipment.

Sections (where practicable)
Heights from floor to floor, ceiling heights and thickness of floors.
Depth of beams.
Height of ridge.
Construction of roof, eaves and verge.
construction of staircase, number of treads and direction, dimensions of rise and going.
Damp proof courses.
Details of window and door sills and heads.

All Elevations
Running measurements to 'pick-up' all door and window openings.
Vertical measurements to 'pick-up' windows, doors, cornices, gutters, ridge etc.
Position of down pipes, gutters hopper heads etc.
Materials of walls and roof.
Position and sizes of chimney stacks, vent pipes etc.
Construction joints.

Generally
Note any defects such as dampness and cause, dry rot and cause, cracks, bulges, recent repairs.

Where other buildings adjoin the site or building under survey, special note should be made of their dimensions, materials, defects, etc.

Take photograhs.

Sketch perspectives of special and unusual details.

Fig. 13.5 Site and building survey check list

Lane & Ralph △ *Architects*

BRIEFING CHECKLIST

PART 3 INFORMATION FROM LOCAL AUTHORITY

Building Regulations
3.01 Name and address of officer concerned.
Chief Building Control Officer, Town Hall

3.02 Obtain copies of application forms and dates including waiting periods. *forms obtained. submit informally to Building Control Officer before making formal submission, then approval likely in 4 weeks.*

3.03 Check what structural information is required.
full calculation required

3.04 Ask for local knowledge of soil conditions.
firm clay

3.05 Building line

3.06 Hoarding control
10 metres from south west boundary

3.07 Any special requirements.
. no

Town Planning
3.08 Name and address of officer concerned.
Chief Development Officer

3.09 Obtain copies of application forms and dates including waiting periods. *Forms obtained. Approval can take 8 weeks after receipt of application*

3.10 Check:

Zoning *industrial*

Floor Space Index, Plot Ration or Density. *no special requirements*

Car Parking requirements *cater for all employees on site No parking space available outside site*

Height restrictions *2 storeys max.*

Access restrictions *Off Pound Road only*

Materials preferences *use of bricks encouraged*

Tree preservation orders *none*

Planting requirements *none*

3.11 Any special requirements *none*

Fig. 13.6 Local authority briefing check list

Lane & Ralph △ *Architects*

FACTORY AND OFFICE BLOCK FOR HENRY ELECTRONICS LTD
STEPHEN'S INDUSTRIAL ESTATE, BOX HILL, EPSOM

AGENDA FOR DESIGN TEAM MEETING NO. 1

29th March 1989

1.00 PERSONNEL / ORGANIZATIONS

1.01 Introduction of people present at meeting.

1.02 Apologies for absence.

1.03 Design team involved in project.

   Architects : Lane & Ralph.

   Quantity Surveyors : Vincent, John & Partners.

   Consulting Structural Engineers : Lewis and Son.

   Consulting Building Services Engineer : John Andrews MCIBS.

   Clerk of Works : C. Robinson.

1.04 Define roles and responsibilities of personnel / organizations.

1.05 Answer questions on fees and conditions of appointment.

1.06 Establish relationships between design team members and client.

2.00 BRIEF

2.01 Background information.

2.02 Briefing and information received to date.

2.03 Further information required from client.

3.00 FEASIBILITY STUDY

3.01 Land survey.

   a) Scope.

   b) Responsibility.

3.02 Soil investigation.

    a) Scope.

    b) Responsibility.

3.03 Statutory and other authorities.

    Town planning.

    Highways.

    Sewers.

    Water.   Define scope of enquiries and responsibilities of team members for enquiries.

    Gas.

    Electricity.

3.04 Cost implications.

    Cost control methods.

    Cost standards and limitations.

    Cost plan.

4.00 **TENDER AND CONTRACT PROCEDURE**

4.01 Tenders.

4.02 Contract.

5.00 **FEASIBILITY REPORT**

5.01 Architect's contribution.

5.02 Quantity surveyor's contribution.

5.03 Consulting structural engineer's contribution.

5.04 Consulting building services engineer's contribution.

5.05 Presentation.

    Written material.

    Drawings.

    Style.

6.00 **PROGRAMME**

6.01 Land survey.

6.02 Soil investigation.

6.03 Meetings with statutory and other authorities.

6.04 Cost implications.

6.05 Submission of draft contributions by design team members.

6.06 Draft report assembled.

6.07 Final report completed.

7.00 **FUTURE MEETINGS**

7.01 Main meetings.

      a) Date. Time. Place.

      b) Persons attending.

7.02 Subsidiary meetings.

      a) Date. Time. Place.

      b) Persons attending.

8.00 **DISTRIBUTION OF MINUTES**

      Agree list.

9.00 **ANY OTHER BUSINESS**

Fig. 13.7 Agenda for design team meeting no. 1

FOUR Completed Copies of this Form and Plans
must be submitted together with **ONE** Copy of
the appropriate Certificate **TO :—**

BOROUGH PLANNING OFFICER
Borough Planning Department
EPSOM & EWELL BOROUGH COUNCIL
P.O. Box 5, Town Hall, The Parade
EPSOM, Surrey   KT18 5BY
Tel No **Epsom 26252**

| EP |

OFFICE USE ONLY

APPLICATION NUMBER

Date received   Date accepted

C/D

**APPLICATION FOR PERMISSION OR APPROVAL
TO DEVELOP LAND ETC — Part 1 All applications**

Town and Country Planning Act 1971

R/NR

FEE DUE £.......................

FEE CHECKED.....................

PLEASE READ THE ACCOMPANYING NOTES FOR APPLICANTS BEFORE COMPLETING ANY PART OF THIS FORM
If extra space is required to answer any question please attach a separate sheet indicating the relevant question(s)

1   Applicant
(In block capitals)

Name   HENRY ELECTRONICS LTD
Address   100 HART ROAD
.... LONDON
.... SWI .... Post Code ....
Tel No

Agent (if any) to whom correspondence should be sent
(In block capitals)

Name   LANE & RALPH, ARCHITECTS
Address   HOGSMILL HOUSE, SARAH'S DRIVE
.... STONELEIGH, EPSOM
.... SURREY .... Post Code ....
Tel No **01-394 1234**

2 (a) Address or location of land
to which application relates

Stephen's Industrial Estate,
Box Hill, Epsom, Surrey

Site must be shown edged RED on the submitted site plan *See note 8*   State site area in Hectares   **3·1**   or Acres

(b) Does the site comprise land registered in accordance with Class 2 of the Community Land (Excepted Development)
Regulations 1976 as being land owned by a builder or developer on 12th September 1974?   State Yes or No   **No**

3   Brief particulars of proposed development, including the purpose(s) for which the land and/or buildings are to be used

Single storey factory of 700 square metres for the assembly
of electronic components, together with a single storey
warehouse of 700 square metres, and a two-storey
office block of 600 square metres.
Parking spaces to be provided for all people employed at
the site, together with lorry parking

4   Particulars of application   *See notes 3 and 4*

Is this application for :—   State Yes or No

(a)	Outline planning permission	**No**
or **(b)**	Full planning permission	**Yes**
or **(c)**	Approval of reserved matters following the grant of outline permission	**No**
or **(d)**	Continuance of use without complying with a condition subject to which planning permission has been granted	**No**
or **(e)**	Permission for the retention of buildings or works constructed, or for the continuance of a use of land instituted before the date of this application	**No**

If **Yes** tick any of the following which are to be considered as part of this
application
1 Siting   2 Design   3 External appearance
4 Means of access   5 Landscaping

If **Yes** state the Date and Number of outline permission
Date _____   Number _____

If **Yes** state the Date and Number of previous permission and identify
the particular condition
Date _____   Number _____
The condition No _____

If **Yes** state the Date when the buildings or works were constructed
or carried out, or the use of the land commenced
Date _____

FORM T.P. 1 (Part 1)   1977

Continued Overleaf

5 Is the development temporary or permanent? .....**Permanent**.... If temporary state for what period. ....

If a previous temporary planning permission exists, state the date and number   Date   Number

6 (a) What is the applicants interest in the land? e.g. Owner, Prospective purchaser, Lessee, etc.   **Owner**...........................

(b) Does the applicant own or control any adjoining land? | **No** | If Yes it must be shown edged BLUE on the submitted site plan

State **Yes** or **No**   *See note 8*

7 If the application is for new residential development, state the following:—

Density in dwellings per hectare/acre		Type (House, Flat, etc)	Number of Garages or garage spaces	
Total number of dwellings		Number of storeys	Number of parking spaces	
Total number of habitable rooms		Total gross floor area of all buildings (Sq metres/Sq feet)		*See note 6*

8   Does the proposed development involve:— **(a)** Construction of a new access to a highway?   **(b)** Alteration of an existing access to a highway?   **(c)** The felling of any trees?

	Vehicular	Pedestrian	Vehicular	Pedestrian	
State **Yes** or **No**					
If **Yes** indicate positions on plan	**Yes**	**Yes**	**No**	**No**	**No**

(d) How will surface water be disposed of?   *Connected to local authority sewer*..........

(e) How will foul sewage be dealt with?   "   "   "   "   "

9 (a) List details of all external building materials to be used if you are submitting them at this stage   *See note 9*

Walls: Golden brown sand faced facing bricks........

Windows and doors: nodised aluminium........

Roofs: Factory — through section aluminium sheeting........

....

(b) List any samples that are being submitted   *Brick. Aluminium for factory roof, "slates" for office roof*.........

....

10 List all drawings, plans, certificates, documents etc; forming part of this application   *See notes 8, 9, 12 and 13*

128/1a   Site plan — Scale 1:200........

2b   Floor and roof plans — Scale 1:100........

3d   Elevations and sections — Scale 1:100........

....

....

11 (a) What is the present use of the land/buildings? If vacant, what was the last use and when did this cease?

Vacant.....

Last use was grazing land........

(b) What buildings are to be demolished?   *Brick store building*...........

If any state gross floor area   (Sq metres/Sq feet)

| *16 sq. M* | ....

12 (a) Are any 'Listed' buildings to be demolished?   *See note 11*   **(b)** Are any 'Listed' buildings to be altered or any non listed buildings in a Conservation Area to be demolished?   State **Yes** or **No** | **No** |

If **Yes** do you wish this application to be treated as an application for Listed Building Consent?   State **Yes** or **No** | **No** |

State **Yes** or **No** | **No** |

NOTE   **1**   Form T.P. 1 (Part 2) should now be completed for all applications involving Industrial, Office, Warehousing, Storage, or Shopping development   **2**   An appropriate Certificate must accompany this application unless you are seeking approval to reserved matters (See notes 12 and 13)   **3**   A separate Form is required for Building Regulation approval (See note 15)

PLEASE ENSURE THIS FORM IS SIGNED AND DATED BEFORE SUBMITTING

I/We hereby apply for planning permission or approval (as the case may be) for the development described herein and shown on the accompanying plans

Signed   *A Lane*   On behalf of   *Henry Electronics Ltd*

Date   *2nd June 1989*   (Insert Applicants name if signed by an Agent)

Fig. 13.8 Town planning application form

COUNCIL OF THE BOROUGH OF EPSOM AND EWELL

**THE BUILDING REGULATIONS 1985
BUILDING ACT 1984**

FOR OFFICE USE ONLY
PLAN NO.
DATE DEPOSITED
FEE CHECKED

To: The Council of the Borough of Epsom and Ewell,
P.O. Box 5, Town Hall, EPSOM, Surrey, KT18 5BY.

I/We hereby give notice of ~~my~~/our intention to:—

Tick as appropriate

- (a) ✓ erect or extend a building;
- (b) make a material alteration to a building;
- (c) provide, extend or materially alter a controlled service or fitting in, or in connection with a building;
- (d) make a material change of use of a building

and deposit the attached drawings and other documents as required by Regulation 13(3)(a) and (b) and Regulation 12 (1-4).

Signed _A Lane_   Date _2nd June 1989_

Name and address of person or persons on whose behalf the work is to be carried out (In block letters please)

HENRY ELECTRONICS LTD,
100 HART ROAD
LONDON
SW1

Telephone No

If signed by agent, give name, profession and address of agent (In block letters please)

LANE & RALPH, ARCHITECTS.
HOGSMILL HOUSE, SARAH'S DRIVE,
STONELEIGH, EPSOM
SURREY

Telephone No 01 - 394 1234

Do the proposals include facilities in respect of a registered disabled person   ~~YES~~/NO

1. Address or location of proposed work	Stephen's Industrial Estate, Box Hill, Epsom Surrey
2. (a) Description of proposed work	Erection on single storey factory and warehouse and two-storey office block
(b) Estimates	
(i) Total Cost	£1,000,000
(ii) Building Regulation Content	£700,000 FEE ENCLOSED £1,217
3. (a) Purpose for which the building/extention will be used	(a) Assembly of electronic components
(b) If existing building state present use	(b)
4. Means of water supply	The Sutton District Water Company
5. Mode of drainage	
(a) Foul water	(a) Layout as shown on drawing no's 128 1a & 2b. Connected to local authority sewer.
(b) Surface water	(b) Layout as shown on drawing no's 128 1a & 2b. Connected to local authority sewer.

NOTES:
(a) This Notice should be completed in duplicate and submitted together with, where applicable, plans and particulars in duplicate in accordance with the provisions of Building Regulation 12(1) to (4) and 13.
(b) Additional information may be requested pursuant to Building Regulation 13(3)(b).

11.11.85
BR1

PLA1/8

Fig. 13.9 Building regulation application form

Lane & Ralph △ *Architects*

Hogsmill House,
Sarah's Drive,
Stoneleigh,
Surrey.

Tel: 01-394 12340
Our ref:
Your ref:

```
Mr O Henry
Henry Electronics Ltd.
100 Hart Road
London SW1
```

```
                                    6th June 1989
```

```
Dear Mr Henry,

Now that you have given us approval of our Scheme Design, I am pleased
to tell you that we are proceeding with our Detail Design Work.

This means that we have reached the stage in the pre-contract part of
the project when any alterations to the brief cannot be made without the
possibility of incurring extra costs and endangering the starting and
completion dates on site.  There is the further complication that any
changes could mean that applications for statutory approvals would have
to be resubmitted, which could also lead to delay and additional costs.
We mention this because, as you are aware, we are working to a very
tight programme, and are anxious to meet your required completion date
for the project, and keep the cost within your cost limits.

Yours sincerely,
```

A Lane

```
A. Lane
```

Fig. 13.10 Typical letter sent to client at start of detail design stage

Lane & Ralph △ *Architects*

CHECK LIST FOR ORGANIZATION OF PRODUCTION INFORMATION

1.00 **LIST OF DRAWINGS AND SCHEDULES TO BE PREPARED**
N.B. Content of each drawing to be listed, with scales.

1.01 Location drawings.

    a) Block plans.

    b) Site plans.

    c) Floor plans.

    d) Foundation plans.

    e) Roof plans.

    f) Sections.

    g) Elevations.

1.02 Assembly drawings.

    a) Use of standard drawings.   N.B. Quote detail numbers.

       External walls.

       Wall openings.

       Eaves details.

       Parapet details.

       Roof lights.

       Internal walls.

       Internal wall openings.

       Suspended ceilings.

    b) Non standard drawings. N.B. List each drawing.

1.03 Component drawings.

    a) Use of standard drawings. N.B. Quote detail numbers.

       Windows.

       Doors.

    b) Non standard drawings. N.B. List each drawing.

1.04 Schedules

   a) Windows.

   b) Doors.

   c) Ironmongery.

   d) Manholes.

1.05 Structural drawings.

   a) Structural steel general arrangements.

   b) Structural steel details.

   c) Reinforced concrete general arrangements.

   d) Reinforced concrete details.

   e) Other drawings.

   f) Schedules.

1.06 Building engineering services drawings.

   a) Drainage.

   b) Discharge pipework.

   c) Electrical.

   d) Water.

   e) Heating and a.c.

   f) Other.

2.00 **DRAWING PROCEDURES**

2.01 Standard sheet sizes.

2.02 Scales.

2.03 Title panel/job title/job number/numbering system.

2.04 Annotation style - stencil or freehand.

2.05 Use of computers.

2.06 Production of copy negatives.

   List who is to prepare and receive negatives.

```
3.00  REFERENCING

3.01  Grid

3.02  Floor levels.

3.03  Floor numbers.

3.04  Room numbers.

3.05  North point.

4.00  AGREE TOLERANCES

4.01  Structure.

4.02  Services.

5.00  SPECIFICATIONS

5.01  Method.

5.02  Contributions from consultants.

5.03  Contributions from sub-contractors and suppliers.

6.00  OUTSTANDING INFORMATION REQUIRED

6.01  Client.

6.02  Consultants (structural engineering).

6.03  Consultants (building engineering services).

6.04  Sub-contractors and suppliers.

6.05  Agree timetable.
```

Fig. 13.11 Check list for organisation of production information

Lane & Ralph △ *Architects*

DRAWINGS CHECK LIST

1.00 **GENERAL**

1.01 All information applicable in Title Panel must be completed.

1.02 Revision letters and descriptions.

1.03 Cross references to other drawings, and general notes.

1.04 North Point.

1.05 Datum for levels.

2.00 **SITE AND LAYOUT PLANS**

2.01 Setting out dimensions.

2.02 Existing and new levels.

2.03 Landscaping (e.g. trees to be retained or removed, fences and hedges to be removed, ditches filled in, pavings etc.).

2.04 Building line.

2.05 Fences, gates and new accesses.

2.06 Public footpaths and rights of way.

2.07 Adjacent buildings.

2.08 Road names.

2.09 Paths.

2.10 Sewer mains and invert levels.

2.11 Gas main.

2.12 Electricity.

2.13 Telephone.

2.14 Water supply.

2.15 Drainage.

3.00 **FLOOR PLANS**

3.01 Dimensions (including wall thicknesses).

3.02 Floor areas.

3.03 Floor levels.

3.04 Section lines.

3.05 Room names and/or numbers.

3.06 Floor finishes.

3.07 Beams over (dotted).

Rooflights over (dotted).

3.08 Services ducts.

3.09 Flues.

3.10 Vertical damp proof courses.

3.11 Built in furniture.

3.12 Door numbers, swings.

3.13 Window numbers.

3.14 Stairs (number treads, show directions up and/or down).

3.15 Roof space access.

3.16 Expansion joints.

4.00 **ROOF PLANS**

4.01 Dimensions.

4.02 Falls.

4.03 Gutters and falls.

4.04 Rainwater outlets.

4.05 Roof finishes.

4.06 Parapet copings.

4.07 **Maximum** and **minimum** screed thicknesses.

4.08 Flues.

4.09 Vents.

4.10 Rooflights.

4.11 Lightning conductors.

4.12 Expansion joints.

5.00 **SECTIONS**

5.01 Structural and finished floor levels.

5.02 Floor to ceiling (or floor to floor) heights.

5.03 Vertical dimensions.

5.04 Foundation dimensions.

5.05 Ground level (existing and finished).

5.06 Damp proof courses and membranes.

5.07 Roof pitches.

5.08 Tanking.

6.00 **ELEVATIONS**

6.01 Floor lines (related to datum).

6.02 Windows including opening types.

6.03 Sill heights.

6.04 Soil and vent pipes.

6.05 Rainwater pipes and gutters.

6.06 Rainwater heads.

6.07 Expansion joints to brickwork etc.

6.08 Window numbers.

7.00 **FOUNDATION PLANS**

7.01 Dimensions, levels.

7.02 Reinforcement to concrete.

7.03 Position of walls.

7.04 Damp proof courses.

7.05 Expansion joints.

8.00 **DRAINAGE PLANS**

8.01 Sewer main (type, i.e. foul, combined etc.).

8.02 Postion of sanitary fittings.

8.03 Soil and waste pipe layout.

8.04 Inspection chamber and manhole positions, sizes, inverts.

8.05 Vent pipes.

8.06 Gulleys.

8.07 Grease traps.

8.08 Rodding eyes.

8.09 Cesspool.

8.10 Soakaways.

8.11 Septic tank.

8.12 Rainwater pipes.

8.13 Interceptors.

9.00 **ELECTRICAL SERVICES**

9.01 Lighting points.

9.02 Power points.

9.03 Switches.

9.04 Rising main.

9.05 Meter cupboard.

9.06 Bell installation.

9.07 Alarm system.

10.00 **WATER SERVICES**

10.01 Rising main.

10.02 Point of entry first stop cock.

10.03 Cold water storage tank.

10.04 Hot water cylinder.

10.05 H.w. expansion tank.

10.06 Stop cocks.

10.07 Taps.

10.08 Sanitary fittings.

10.09 Fire fighting equipment.

10.10 Overflow pipes.

10.11 Drain cocks.

11.00 **HEATING AND A.C. SERVICES**

11.01 Pipe work.

11.02 Ductwork.

11.03 Boilers.

11.04 Tanks.

11.05 Pumps.

11.06 Terminal units.

11.07 A.c. plant.

11.08 Louvres.

Fig. 13.12 Drawing check list

Lane & Ralph △ *Architects*

Tel: 01-394 12340
Our ref:
Your ref:

Hogsmill House,
Sarah's Drive,
Stoneleigh,
Surrey.

4th July 1989

Porter Construction Ltd.
77 Pembroke Road
Kingston
Surrey

Dear Sirs,

FACTORY AND OFFICE BLOCK, STEPHEN'S INDUSTRIAL ESTATE, BOX HILL.

We will shortly be inviting tenders for the above project, and are
writing to ask if you are interested in being considered for inclusion
in the tender list.

If you wish to be considered will you please supply us with the
following information by the 13th July.

1. Minimum and maximum value of individual contracts your company
    is prepared to undertake.

2. Type of contract your company is prepared to undertake.

3. What work is normally undertaken by your own company, and what
    work is sub-contracted.

4. The name and address of your company bankers.

5. Details of three contracts undertaken by you during the past
    three years as follows.

    a) Address of contract.
    b) Client's name and address.
    c) Type of project.
    d) Approximate contract value.
    e) Start and completion dates.
    f) Architect's name and address.
    g) Quantity surveyor's name and address.
    h) Consulting structural engineer's name and address.
    i) Consulting building services engineer's name and address.

Serious consideration will be given to including your name in the tender
list, but failure to do so will in no way mean your company was
considered unsuitable.

Yours faithfully,

A Lane

Arnold Lane.

Fig. 13.13 Letter asking for information from potential tenderers

Lane & Ralph △ *Architects*

Tel: 01-394 12340
Our ref:
Your ref:

Hogsmill House,
Sarah's Drive,
Stoneleigh,
Surrey.

11th July 1989

Brown and Taylor
Chartered Architects
44 Ascham Road
Epsom
Surrey

Dear Sirs,

FACTORY AND OFFICE BLOCK, STEPHEN'S INDUSTRIAL ESTATE, BOX HILL.

We have been informed by Porter Construction Ltd. that they recently completed a contract under your supervision. As we are considering inviting them to tender for an office block and factory development valued at about £1,000,000 we are writing to ask for your opinion as to their suitability for this contract.

We would therefore be most grateful if you would kindly complete the enclosed assessment sheet. All the information supplied by you will be treated in the strictest confidence.

Yours faithfully,

A Lane

Arnold Lane

Fig. 13.14 Letter to referee about potential tenderer

Lane & Ralph △ *Architects*

ASSESSMENT SHEET ON THE SUITABILITY FOR INCLUDING IN A TENDER LIST

Porter Construction Ltd

FOR A *factory and office block, Box Hill, Epsom*

COSTING IN THE REGION OF £ 1,000,000

ITEM	PERFORMANCE Please tick		
	Below Average	Average	Above Average
Performance at pre-contract stage			
Performance of administrative staff during contract period			
Performance of site staff			
Ability to keep to programme			
Abiltiy to meet specified quality standards			
Ability to handle sub-contractors and suppliers			
Co-operation when problems arose			
Performance in meeting completion date			
Co-operation with regard to settlement of claims			

ANY OTHER INFORMATION

FROM : Name

      Address

      Signature
      Date

Fig. 13.15 Assessment sheet on suitability of tenderer

Lane & Ralph △ *Architects*

<u>FACTORY AND OFFICE BLOCK, STEPHEN'S INDUSTRIAL ESTATE, BOX HILL</u>

<u>AGENDA FOR DESIGN TEAM MEETING NO. 3</u>

14TH MAY 1989

1.00 **PERSONNEL / ORGANIZATION**
1.01 Introduction of people present at meeting.
1.02 Apologies for absence.
1.03 List of personnel / organizations not present but with whom
    contact will need to be made at this stage of the project.

2.00 **OUTSTANDING BUSINESS FROM PREVIOUS MEETING**
2.01 Approval of scheme by client's insurers.
2.02 Client's decision on list of tenderers.
2.03 Client's decision-placing of advance order for steel.
2.04 Settlement of fee accounts.

3.00 **PRODUCTION INFORMATION**
3.01 Confirm information required to date has been received and
    is correct.
3.02 Record question and answer sheets received.
3.03 Confirm any other information / instructions supplied
    since last meeting.
3.04 Agree remaining information required at this stage of
    project, with dates.
3.05 Confirm last date on which quantity surveyor can accept
    further information for including in B.Q.
3.06 Any other queries on production information.

4.00 **BILLS OF QUANTITIES**
4.01 Confirm format and number of bills required.
4.02 Agree timetable for completion and printing of bills.
4.03 Any other queries on bills.

5.00 **TENDER STAGE**
5.01 Action to be taken on list of tenderers.
5.02 Action to be taken on nominated sub-contractors and
    suppliers.
5.03 Tender programme.
5.04 Any other queries on tender stage.

6.00 **MEETING TO DISCUSS SITE STAFF**
6.01 People attending.
6.02 Date and place of meeting.
6.03 Any other queries on site staff.

7.00 **FUTURE MEETINGS**
7.01 People attending.
7.02 Date and Place.

8.00 **ANY OTHER BUSINESS**

Fig. 13.16 Agenda for design team meeting at bills of quantities stage

Lane & Ralph △ *Architects*

CHECK LIST FOR USE AT STAGES G - BILLS OF QUANTITIES

1.00 **CLIENT** Check the following from client have been incorporated
1.01 Written instructions.
1.02 Telephone and verbal instruction - confirm to client.

2.00 **STATUTORY APPROVALS** - Check the following have been incorporated.
2.01 Town planning requirements.
2.02 Building regulations requirements.
2.03 Fire officer's requirements.
2.04 H & S at W A inspector's requirements.
2.05 Other statutory requirements.
2.06 Check all consents have been received.

3.00 **CONSULTANTS** - Check work shown on architect's drawings have been
incorporated.
3.01 Structural engineers.
3.02 Building services engineers.
3.03 Others.

4.00 **ARCHITECTS** - Cross check information on the following.
4.01 Component drawings against relevant assembly drawings.
4.02 Assembly drawings against relevant location drawings.

5.00 **SCHEDULES** - Check against the following drawings.
5.01 Architect's drawings.
5.02 Structural engineer's drawings.
5.03 Building services engineer's drawings.
5.04 Others.

6.00 **SPECIFICATIONS** - Check against the following drawings.
6.01 Architect's drawings.
6.02 Structural engineer's drawings.
6.03 Building services engineer's drawings.
6.04 Others.

7.00 **QUESTIONS AND ANSWERS SHEETS** - Check they are :
7.01 Included in bills.
7.02 Incorporated in drawings.

8.00 **TOTAL INFORMATION USE FOR BILLS OF QUANTITIES** - Record all
information supplied and cross-check there is no conflict of
information.
8.01 Architect's drawings, schedules and specifications.
8.02 Structural engineer's drawings, schedules and specifications.
8.03 Building services engineer's drawings, schedules and
specifications.

9.00 **PRIME COST AND PROVISIONAL SUMS**
9.01 Prime cost sums.
9.02 Provisional sums.

10.00 **LATE INFORMATION**
10.01 List all items.
10.02 Cover with draft architect's instructions.

Fig. 13.17 Check list for use at bills of quantities stage

Lane & Ralph △ *Architects*

<u>FACTORY AND OFFICE BLOCK, STEPHEN'S INDUSTRIAL ESTATE, BOX HILL</u>

<u>AGENDA FOR MEETING TO DISCUSS SITE SUPERVISORY STAFF</u>

15TH JULY 1989

1.00 **PERSONNEL / ORGANIZATION**
1.01 Record people present.
1.02 Apologies for absence.

2.00 **APPOINTMENT OF SITE STAFF**
2.01 Decision to appoint clerk of works.
     Consider appointment for part of contract / part-time of :
2.02 Resident engineer - structural.
2.03 Resident engineer - building engineering services.

3.00 **ROLES**
3.01 Clerk of works.
3.02 Resident engineer structural - if appointed.
3.03 Resident engineer building engineering services - if appointed.

4.00 **CONDITIONS OF SERVICE**
     Consider salary/perks, hours, responsibilities.
4.01 Clerk of works.
4.02 Resident engineer - structural.
4.03 Resident engineer - building engineering services.

5.00 **SELECTION**
     Consider selection, recruitment, interviews.
5.01 Clerk of works.
5.02 Resident engineer - structural.
5.03 Resident engineer - building engineering services.

6.00 **LINE OF COMMAND**
     Consider organisation and command of
6.01 Clerk of works.
6.02 Resident engineer - structural.
6.03 Resident engineer - building engineering services.

7.00 **ANY OTHER BUSINESS**

Fig. 13.18 Agenda of meeting to discuss appointment of site staff

Lane & Ralph △ *Architects*

Tel: 01-394 12340
Our ref:
Your ref:

Hogsmill House,
Sarah's Drive,
Stoneleigh,
Surrey.

18th July 1989

Dear Sirs,

FACTORY AND OFFICE BLOCK, STEPHEN'S INDUSTRIAL ESTATE, BOX HILL.

We are preparing a list of tenderers for the construction of the above job and need to know whether you wish to submit a tender.

We give below information relevant to the tender.

GENERAL JOB DESCRIPTION: Single storey factory with two-storey office block.

JOB LOCATION: Stephen's Industrial Estate, Box Hill, Epsom.

EMPLOYER: Henry Electronics Ltd.

QUANTITY SURVEYOR: Vincent, John & Partners.

CONSULTING STRUCTURAL ENGINEERS: Lewis & Son.

CONSULTING BUILDING SERVICES ENGINEERS John Andrew M.C.I.B.S.

APPROXIMATE COST RANGE: £800,000 to £1,000,000.

FORM OF CONTRACT: J.C.T. private edition with quantities.

ANTICIPATED DATE FOR COMMENCING WORK: 17th October 1989.

ANTICIPATED DATE FOR COMPLETION: 18th September 1990.

ANTICIPATED DATE FOR SENDING TENDER DOCUMENTS: 15th August 1989.

ANTICIPATED DATE FOR RETURNING TENDER DOCUMENTS: 19th September 1989.

Please let us know by the 25th July whether you wish to be included in the list of tenderers. Your acceptance will indicate your agreement to submit a tender in accordance with the R.I.B.A. Code of Practice for Single-Stage Selective Tendering.

Yours faithfully,

A Lane

A. Lane

Fig. 13.19 Letter to potential tenderer

```
TO :

Lane & Ralph
Architects
Hogsmill House
Sarah's Drive
Stoneleigh
Surrey



Dear Sirs,

FACTORY AND OFFICE BLOCK, STEPHEN'S INDUSTRIAL ESTATE, BOX HILL.

We hereby agree to execute and complete the whole of the works for the
above job, strictly in accordance with the drawings, schedules,
specifications, bills of quantities and conditions of contract supplied
to us for the sum of ................................................

.....................................................£.............

within a period of .... weeks of being given possession of the site.

We enclose the schedule of rates upon which our tender is based.  Our
tender will remain open for acceptance for a period of ......weeks.

Yours faithfully,



Signature...............................

NAME....................................

ADDRESS.................................

       .................................

       .................................

DATE..................
```

Fig. 13.20 Form of tender

Lane & Ralph △ *Architects*

Tel: 01-394 12340
Our ref:
Your ref:

Hogsmill House,
Sarah's Drive,
Stoneleigh,
Surrey.

15th August 1989

Porter Construction Ltd.
77 Pembroke Road
Kingston
Surrey

Dear Sirs,

FACTORY AND OFFICE BLOCK, STEPHEN'S INDUSTRIAL ESTATE, BOX HILL.

Further to our enquiry dated the 15th July regarding your willingness to tender for the above job, and your acceptance dated the 18th July, we enclose the following documents which you will need to prepare your tender.

1. Two copies of the bills of quantities.
2. One copy of the following drawings and schedules.
   Drawings no. 128/1a, 2b, 3d, 4a, 5, 6a, 7b, 9a.
   Schedules 128/5, 6, 7.
3. Two copies of the form of tender.
4. An addressed envelope for the return of your tender.
   An addressed envelope for the return of your priced bills of quantities.

Your tender is required to reach our office at the above address by 9.00 a.m. 19th September 1989.

Please confirm the safe arrival of this letter and documents, and your intention to submit a bona fide tender in accordance with the R.I.B.A. Code of Practice for Single-Stage Selective Tendering by returning and signing the enclosed acknowledgement form.

You are advised to inspect the site. Please contact the job architect, Maureen White, tel: 01-394-12340, to make the necessary arrangements.

Additional production drawings are available for inspection, by arrangement. Please contact the job architect to agree an appointment to study this additional information.

Yours faithfully,

A. Ralph

Arnold Ralph

Fig. 13.21 Letter of invitation to tender

```
TO :

Lane & Ralph
Architects
Hogsmill House
Sarah's Drive
Stoneleigh
Surrey



Dear Sirs,

FACTORY AND OFFICE BLOCK, STEPHEN'S INDUSTRIAL ESTATE, BOX HILL.

CONTRACTOR :  PORTER CONSTRUCTION LTD.

I acknowledge on behalf of the above contractor the safe receipt of all
the tender documents listed in the accompanying letter which you sent us
in connection with the above contract.

I confirm it is our intention to submit a tender by the date requested
in your letter.

SIGNED............................

DESIGNATION.......................

DATE.............
```

Fig. 13.22 Acknowledgement of safe receipt of tender documents

Lane & Ralph △ *Architects*

INITIAL COMPARISON OF TENDERS

PROJECT : Factory and office block, Box Hill, Epsom

TENDERS OPENED : Lane & Ralph's office, Stoneleigh

DATE : 19th September 1989

PLACING	TENDERER	FIXED PRICE SUM	TENDERER'S CONTRACT PERIOD (N.B. Client's preferred period is 48 weeks)	COMMENTS
		£	Weeks	
3	Bain Bros. Ltd	1,050,442	48	Early items are surcharged
2	A. Payne Ltd	1,007,600	46	Labour rates on high side materials rates on low side
1	Porter Construction Ltd	1,002,565	48	
4	Pride Construction Ltd	1,113,450	48	Errors in addition increase price by £35,000
5	Smith and Jones Ltd	1,213,645	52	

Fig. 13.23 Form for initial comparison tenders

Lane & Ralph △ *Architects*

Tel: 01-394 12340
Our ref:
Your ref:

Hogsmill House,
Sarah's Drive,
Stoneleigh,
Surrey.

21st September 1989

Porter Construction Ltd.
77 Pembroke Road
Kingston
Surrey

Dear Sirs,

FACTORY AND OFFICE BLOCK, STEPHEN'S INDUSTRIAL ESTATE, BOX HILL.

We are pleased to inform you that the tenders for the above job were
opened on the 19th September and your tender was placed lowest.

Subject to a final check being made, and a proper form of contract being
entered into, we are recommending to our client that your tender be
accepted.

A full list of all tenders received will be sent to you at a later date.

Yours faithfully,

A Lane

Arnold Lane

Fig. 13.24 Letter to successful tenderer

Lane & Ralph △ *Architects*

Tel: 01-394 12340
Our ref:
Your ref:

Hogsmill House,
Sarah's Drive,
Stoneleigh,
Surrey.

21st September 1989

A Payne Ltd.
Rush Way
Dorking
Surrey

Dear Sirs,

FACTORY AND OFFICE BLOCK, STEPHEN'S INDUSTRIAL ESTATE, BOX HILL.

We regret to inform you that the tenders for the above job were opened
on the 19th September and that your price was not the lowest submitted.

Although you were unsuccessful on this occasion we wish to thank you for
submitting a tender and ensure you that you will not be precluded from
being considered for future tenders.

A full list of all tenders received will be sent to you at a later date.

Yours faithfully,

A Lane

Arnold Lane

Fig. 13.25 Letter to unsuccessful tenderer

Lane & Ralph △ *Architects*

CHECK LIST OF INFORMATION TO BE GIVEN TO THE CLIENT AT THE
PROJECT PLANNING STAGE

1.00 **COST CONTROL**
1.01 Only the architect can instruct the contractor – the client must
     act through him.
1.02 Procedure for varying works.
1.03 Procedure for granting an extension of time.
1.04 Procedure for payment of works.
1.05 Arrangements for site meetings.
1.06 Arrangements for site visits
1.07 Arrangements for reporting on state of job, in respect of progress,
     costs, and other factors.

2.00 **CLIENT'S ROLE AS EMPLOYER CONFIRMED**
2.01 Duty to give contractor possession of site.
2.02 Rights as to assignment of contract.
2.03 Powers to employ others if contractor does not comply with
     instructions.
2.04 Obligations regarding insurance.
2.05 Rights and duties in respect of contractor's bankruptcy.
2.06 No liability to nominated sub-contractors.
2.07 Powers and duties concerning certificates.
2.08 Rights regarding 'finds'.
2.09 Situation regarding arbitration.

3.00 **ARCHITECT'S ROLE EXPLAINED**
3.01 Role as agent.
3.02 Quasi-judicial role.
3.03 Custody of contract documents.
3.04 Powers and duties regarding prime cost sums and provisional sums.
3.05 Duty to issue certificates – to be honoured within 14 days.
3.06 Duty to issue certificate of practical completion.
3.07 Powers regarding non-completion.
3.08 Duties relating to nominated sub-contractors and suppliers.

4.00 **CLERK OF WORKS ROLE EXPLAINED**
4.01 Definition of duties, particularly to act under architect as
     inspector of works, but is servant of client.
4.02 Limitations.
4.03 Duties regarding 'finds'.
4.04 Arrangements for payment of salary.

5.00 **QUANTITY SURVEYOR'S ROLE EXPLAINED**
5.01 Duties regarding variations, provisional sums, and prime cost sums.
5.02 Duties relating to costs involved in 'finds'.

6.00 **CONSULTANT'S ROLES EXPLAINED**
6.01 Structural engineering.
6.02 Building services engineer.

Fig. 13.26 Check list of information to be given to client at project stage

Lane & Ralph △ *Architects*

Tel: 01-394 12340
Our ref:
Your ref:

Hogsmill House,
Sarah's Drive,
Stoneleigh,
Surrey.

3rd October 1989

Structural Steel Constructions (Polegate) Ltd.
Radcliffe Road
Polegate
Sussex

Dear Sirs,

FACTORY AND OFFICE BLOCK, STEPHEN'S INDUSTRIAL ESTATE, BOX HILL.

Further to your tender for the supply and fixing of the structural
steelwork to the factory building, we wish to inform you that we have
requested the contractor to accept your tender dated the 6th July for
the amount stated, inclusive of 2½% discount for payment within the
stipulated time.

We enclose for your information a list of the tenderers with their
tender amounts.

Yours faithfully,

A Lane

Arnold Lane

Fig. 13.27 Letter to successful sub-contractor

Lane & Ralph △ *Architects*

Hogsmill House,
Sarah's Drive,
Stoneleigh,
Surrey.

Tel: 01-394 12340
Our ref:
Your ref:

2nd October 1989

Dear Sirs,

FACTORY AND OFFICE BLOCK, STEPHEN'S INDUSTRIAL ESTATE, BOX HILL.

Further to your tender for the supply and fixing of the structural
steelwork for the above project, we wish to inform you that you were not
successful in this instance.

We shall however be pleased to send you enquiries for our future
projects.

We enclose for your information a list of the tenderers, with their
amounts.

Yours faithfully,

A Lane

Arnold Lane

Fig. 13.28 Letter to unsuccessful sub-contractor

Lane & Ralph △ *Architects*

Tel: 01-394 12340
Our ref:
Your ref:

Hogsmill House,
Sarah's Drive,
Stoneleigh,
Surrey.

10th October 1989

Porter Construction Ltd.
77 Pembroke Road
Kingston
Surrey

Dear Sirs,

FACTORY AND OFFICE BLOCK, STEPHEN'S INDUSTRIAL ESTATE, BOX HILL.

This is to confirm that the above site will be handed over to you at
9 a.m. on Monday 17th October.

From this date until the completion of the contract you will be
responsible for the security of the site, for the safety of anyone
entering the site, and for the security and safety of all partially and
completed buildings, and all materials on the site.

We wish to draw your attention to the following special conditions that
apply to the control of this site.

1. The footpath running alongside the north west boundary to the site
    is a public right of way and must be maintained at all times.

2. Care must be taken not to damage the buildings immediately adjoining
    the south east boundary.

3. The mature oak tree near the centre of the site must be protected
    against damage from building operations.

Yours faithfully,

A Lane

Arnold Lane

Fig. 13.29 Letter regarding handing over site to contractor

Lane & Ralph △ *Architects*

ARCHITECT'S GENERAL CHECK LIST DURING OPERATIONS ON SITE

1.00 GENERAL
1.01 Follow Site Inspection Check List.
1.02 Check that materials on site conform to specification and are undamaged. N.B. Instructions are to be issued for removal of unsuitable materials.
1.03 Approve sample of materials and workmanship.
1.04 Issue instructions to remove unsatisfactory items of work.
1.05 Keep record of each site visit. Take all necessary action. Maintain records.
1.06 Check site manager is permanently on site, and that contractor's site supervision is adequate.

2.00 DRAWINGS
2.01 Check drawings are sent to contractor so as to meet the requirements of his agreed programme.
2.02 Check that drawings have been received by the contractor.
2.03 Check that drawings are revised to incorporate all variations and instructions.
2.04 Check the clerk of works in maintaining a set of 'as-built' drawings.

3.00 PROGRAMME AND PROGRESS
3.01 Check work is proceeding as agreed programme.
3.02 Check that progress photographs are being taken at regular intervals.

4.00 EXTENSION OF TIME
4.01 Consider claims from contractor for an extension of time.
4.02 Where justified, issue notice of extension of time within the contractual time limits.

5.00 NOMINATED SUB-CONTRACTORS AND SUPPLIERS
5.01 Check that any outstanding nominations are made in adequate time to suit the agreed programme.
5.02 Check that unsuccessful sub-contractors and suppliers have been notified of results.
5.03 Check instructions regarding sub-contractors and suppliers have been issued to contractor.
5.04 Check that contractor is not waiting for drawings / information from sub-contractors or suppliers.
5.05 Check that sub-contractors and suppliers are not waiting for drawings / information from architects.

6.00 VARIATIONS AND INSTRUCTIONS
6.01 Check that agreed variations and instructions have been formalized by issue of appropriate standard forms.

7.00 CERTIFICATES
7.01 Issue all certificates in the strictest accordance with contract.

8.00 **PAYMENTS**
8.01 Check that payment has been made for work included in certificates, including cost of instructions and variations. N.B. If the client is in default, notify him, by recorded delivery, of the consequences.
8.02 Check thay payments are being made to sub-contractors and suppliers, where such sums have been included in the certificates for that purpose.
8.03 Arrange for client to pay sub-contractors and suppliers directly, where contractor is failing to meet his contractual obligations.
8.04 Issue the appropriate certificates in cases where necessary, due to sub-contractors or suppliers not meeting their contractual obligations.

9.00 **DETERMINATION OF CONTRACT**
9.01 Take required action if the client wishes the contract with the contractor to be terminated, and such action is justified.
9.02 Consult the client, and his legal advisors, if the contractor requests that the contract be terminated.

10.00 **FEEDBACK**
10.01 Record with notes and sketches any aspect of the design and construction of which account should be taken in future projects. File for future use.
10.02 Record any aspect of administrative work of which account should be taken in future projects. File for future use.

Fig. 13.30 General check list during site operations

Lane & Ralph △ *Architects*

SITE INSPECTION CHECK LIST

1.0 **TEMPORARY WORKS**
1.01 Suitable siting of temporary buildings, huts, etc.
1.02 Suitable storage of materials - protection, security.
1.03 Suitable protection of finished work.
1.04 Rights of way unobstructed.
1.05 Suitable protection of trees etc. which are to be preserved.
1.06 Satisfactory boundary hoardings, fencing.
1.07 Setting out correct.
1.08 Bench marks correct.
1.09 Sample panels all right.
1.10 Topsoil spoil heaps all right.

2.0 **DEMOLITIONS**
2.01 Scope of work all right.
2.02 Temporary supports all right.
2.03 Avoidance of nuisance, danger to adjoining sites, public.
2.04 Items specified to be retained are being retained.

3.0 **SUB-STRUCTURE**
3.01 Check nature of subsoil compared to trial pits / boreholes.
3.02 Dimensions of excavations correct.
3.03 Safety in excavations being achieved.
3.04 De-watering procedures all right.
3.05 Adjoining sites and buildings not endangered by excavations.
3.06 Suitable quality of hardcore.
3.07 Suitable quality of blinding.
3.08 Correct placing of reinforcement, including cover.
3.09 Suitable quality of concrete.
3.10 Correct concrete dimensions.
3.11 Damp proof membranes and tanking all right.
3.12 Ducts through structure correctly sized and positioned.
3.13 Piling work all right - as drawings / specifications.
3.14 Backfilling all right - material and compaction.

4.0 **DRAINAGE**
4.01 General layout / setting out correct.
4.02 Inverts and gradients correct.
4.03 Drain bedding all right.
4.04 Drain jointing all right.
4.05 Manholes materials and workmanship all right - base, walls, cover.

5.0 **STRUCTURAL STEELWORK**
5.01 Setting out correct.
5.02 Size of members correct.
5.03 Connections all right.
5.04 Frame square, plumb and level.
5.05 Corrosion protection - priming.

6.0 **IN-SITU REINFORCED CONCRETE**
6.01 Setting out correct.
6.02 Size of members correct.

6.03 Formwork correct and will give required surface finish to concrete.
6.04 Location of reinforcement correct, including cover.
6.05 Size of reinforcement correct.
6.06 Formwork clean.
6.07 Reinforcement clean.
6.08 Openings, holes, fixings, water bars, correctly positioned.
6.09 Striking programme correct.

7.0 **PRECAST REINFORCED CONCRETE**
7.01 Setting out, size and shape of members correct.
7.02 Finish correct.
7.03 Members have not been damaged during transit of erection.
7.04 Openings, holes fixings, in correct positions.

8.0 **BRICK AND BLOCK WALLING**
8.01 General setting out correct.
8.02 Walls of correct thickness.
8.03 Openings in correct positions.
8.04 Expansion joints in correct positions.
8.05 Work as sample panels - bricks, blocks, mortar colour, joints.
8.06 D.p.cs correct - materials, positions.
8.07 Wall and other ties - correct type and spacings, clean.
8.08 Cavities kept clean.
8.09 Lintels - correct type and bedding.
8.10 Correct reinforcement in calculated brick / blockwork.
8.11 Sliding joint provided.

9.0 **CARPENTRY AND JOINERY**
9.01 Timber free from defects.
9.02 Timber members of correct size.
9.03 Timber members in correct positions and spacings.
9.04 Timber members correctly fixed and jointed.
9.05 Members primed, protected with preservative.
9.06 Joinery members correctly fixed.
9.07 Weather mouldings, throatings provided.
9.08 Wrot faces provided where required.

10.0 **WALL AND ROOF CLADDING**
10.01 Correct general extent of work, position of openings.
10.02 Correct materials - outer sheeting, insulation, vapour barrier, lining.
10.03 Correct arrangement of materials.
10.04 Laps, joints, correctly positioned.
10.05 Fixings - correct types and spacings.
10.06 Flashings, trim, weathermoulds, cappings - correct types, positions.
10.07 Mastic provided where specified.
10.08 Prevention of electrolytic action.
10.09 Curtain wall members - correct type, colour, dimensions.
10.10 Curtain wall panels - correct type, colour, dimensions.
10.11 Finished construction weatherproof.

11.0 **METALWORK**
11.01 Correct type, colour, size of items.
11.02 Correct fixing of items.
11.03 Protection against rust provided.
11.04 Isolation from corrosive materials provided.
11.05 External items weatherproof.

12.0 **ROOFING**
12.01 Correct falls / pitches provided.
12.02 Outlets provided at lowest points.
12.03 Materials as specified - colour, size, appearance.
12.04 Insulation, vapour barrier provided in correct position, order.
12.05 Skirtings as specified to flat roofs.
12.06 Flashings as specified to flat roofs, including wall chases.
12.07 Correct treatment to ridges and verges of pitched roofs.
12.08 Correct drips, gutters provided.
12.09 All roofs weathertight.

13.0 **DISCHARGE PIPEWORK AND SANITARY FITTINGS**
13.01 Sanitary fittings as specified provided in correct locations.
13.02 Vertical pipes - located, fixed, jointed correctly.
13.03 Horizontal pipes - located, fixed, jointed correctly.
13.04 Horizontal pipes laid to correct falls.
13.05 Traps correctly located.
13.06 Accesses, rodding eyes provided.
13.07 Pipe testing.

14.0 **HEATING AND HOT WATER INSTALLATION**
14.01 Plant items as specified, correctly located.
14.02 Flues as specified, correctly located.
14.03 Pipe sizes and runs as drawings.
14.04 Valves - types and positions as specified.
14.05 Pipework insulation provided.
14.06 Pipes correctly labelled and identified.

15.0 **COLD WATER AND SPRINKLER INSTALLATION**
15.01 Plant items as specified, correctly located.
15.02 Pipe sizes and runs as drawings.
15.03 Frost protection provided.
15.04 Valves - types and positions as specified.
15.05 Draining facility provided.
15.06 Pipes correctly labelled and identified.
15.07 Sprinkler heads given protection against paint, dust.

16.0 **AIR CONDITIONING AND VENTILATION**
16.01 Plant items as specified, correctly located.
16.02 Duct sizes and runs as drawings.
16.03 Access provided to ducts.
16.04 Louvres provided as specification.

17.0 **ELECTRICAL INSTALLATIONS**
17.01 Plant items as specified, correctly located.
17.02 Points, outlets, switches, as specified, correctly located.
17.03 Specified cables, correctly run.

17.04 Installation earthed.
17.05 Switchgear identified and labelled.
17.06 Lightning conductor installation correct.
17.07 Communication installation correct.

18.0 **FLOOR FINISHES**
18.01 Materials as specified provided in correct location.
18.02 Screeds of correct type and quality of finish.
18.03 Other bases all right.
18.04 Accurate falls to channels, gullies.
18.05 Setting out correct.
18.06 Standard of finishes all right. Check under final lighting.
18.07 Skirtings, covers all right.
18.03 Junctions between different finishes all right.

19.0 **PLASTERING AND WALL TILING**
19.01 Background true and dry enough.
19.02 Metal beads properly fixed.
19.03 Undercoats ready for bonding - scratching.
19.04 Plaster finish all right. Arrises, openings, corners.
19.05 Filling and scrimming of plasterboard joints.
19.06 Regular joints - horizontally and vertically to glazed tiling.
19.07 Treatment at external angles. Top of tiling all right.

20.0 **SUSPENDED CEILINGS**
20.01 Suspension system at correct height.
20.02 Suspension system correct type, framing arrangement.
20.03 Type of tiles, panels as specified.
20.04 Correct setting out of tiles, panels.
20.05 Lights, grilles, access panels, correctly located.
20.06 Provision for services items - electrical, fire protection.
20.07 Correct finish at walls, head of windows, curtain walling.

21.0 **PROPRIETARY PARTITIONS**
21.01 Partitions correctly located.
21.02 Type of partition as specified.
21.03 Doors, openings, correctly located.
21.04 Suitable fixings at base, head, ends.
21.05 Provision for services items - electrical, fire protection.
21.06 Correct junctions with other elements.

22.0 **GLAZING**
22.01 Glass as specified.
22.02 Glass free from defects.
22.03 Facility for slight movement.
22.04 Putty, glazing beads all right.

23.0 **PAINTING AND DECORATING**
23.01 Correct preparation of surface, freedom from damp.
23.02 Paint of type specified, correct 'thickness'.
23.03 Number of coats as specified.
23.04 Finished work free from 'runs', brush marks.
23.05 Paper wall covering of type specified.
23.06 Wall covering joints all right, openings, skirtings, head.

23.07 General standard of finish acceptable. Check under final lighting.

24.0 **IRONMONGERY**
24.01 All ironmongery, furniture, supplied as schedules.
24.02 All items fixed, correct no. of screws.
24.03 Latches, locks, bolts open correctly.
24.04 Door springs, closers operate correctly.
24.05 Correct number of keys.
24.06 Doors, windows, open easily, not in need of adjustment.

25.0 **CLEANING DOWN**
25.01 Floors scrubbed, free from paint splashes.
25.02 Painted surfaces clean, free from faults.
25.03 Glass cleaned, undamaged.
25.04 Sanitary fittings clean, undamaged.
25.05 Lighting fittings clean, undamaged.
25.06 Switch plates, ironmongery, door / window furniture clean.
25.07 Rooms, areas, generally immaculate.

Fig. 13.31 Site inspection check list

Lane & Ralph △ *Architects*

JOB FACTORY AND OFFICE BLOCK, BOX HILL, EPSOM

DATE 25/11/1989

CONTRACTOR PORTER CONSTRUCTION LTD   WEEK NO. 6

LABOUR ON SITE	MON	TUE	WED	THU	FRI	TOTAL	COMMENTS
Labourers	5	5	4	5	4	23	
Bricklayers	5	5	5	4	4	23	
Structural steelworkers	4	4	4	4	4	20	
Carpenters					2	2	
	14	14	13	13	14	68	

DELAY CAUSED BY	MON	TUE	WED	THU	FRI	TOTAL	COMMENTS
Heavy Rain	5	3				8	
TOTAL HOURS LOST	5	3				8	

	DATE	WEEK NO.
START	17/10/89	1
ORIGINALLY AGREED COMPLETION	18/9/90	48
EXTENSION GRANTED OF WEEKS GIVING REVISED COMPLET.	25/9/90	49
SITE MANAGER'S PRESENT ESTIMATE OF COMPLETION	25/9/90	49

PROBLEMS ON SITE FOR CONTRACTOR'S OWN LABOUR ITEMS
Difficulty likely in maintaining required number of bricklayers

PROBLEMS ON SITE FOR SUB-CONTRACTORED WORK
Roof cladders (factory building) have not yet confirmed they can commence on site when required

DRAWINGS AND INFORMATION RECEIVED
drawing no. 124/2c

DRAWINGS AND INFORMATION REQUIRED
Details of door no's 24 and 32 at junction with steel columns

MATERIALS DELIVERED
Facing bricks. Concrete blocks.   More structural steel items

VISITORS
Mr. Henry (WED.) Mr. Reason H&S.W.A. Inspect (FRI)

OTHER MATTERS   SIGNED C.Robinson
                                       DATE 25/11/89

Fig. 13.32 Clerk of works weekly site report

Lane & Ralph △ *Architects*

AGENDA OF SITE (ARCHITECT'S PROGRESS) MEETING NO.2

FACTORY AND OFFICE BLOCK, STEPHEN'S INDUSTRIAL ESTATE, BOX HILL

TO BE HELD ON 28TH NOVEMBER 1989

1. Minutes of last meeting.

2. Matters arising and action taken.

3. Weather report since last meeting.

4. Contractor's report.

    a) Labour force on site.

    b) General progress.

    c) Reason for any delays.

    d) Claims arising from delays.

    e) Information received since last meeting.

    f) Queries on architect's instructions and variations.

    g) Information required.

    h) Nominated sub-contractors work.

5. Dayworks.

6. Clerk of works report.

7. Quantity surveyor's report.

8. Structural engineer's report.

9. Building services engineer's report.

10. Contract completion date.

11. Any other business.

12. Date of next meeting.

Fig. 13.33 Agenda of site (architect's progress) meeting

Issued by: Lane & Ralph
address: Hogsmill House, Sarah's Drive, Stoneleigh, Surrey

Employer: Henry Electronics Ltd,
address: 100 4 Hart Road London, SW1

Contractor: Porter Construction Ltd
address: 77 Pembroke Road, Kingston, Surrey

Works: Factory and office block
Situated at: Stephen's Industrial Estate, Box Hill, Epsom

Architect's instruction

Serial no: MW/2

Job reference: AL/124

Issue date: 2/12/1989

Contract dated: 10/10/1989

Under the terms of the above Contract, I/We issue the following instructions:

	Office use: Approx costs	
	£ omit	£ add
Revise positions of door nos from that shown on drawing no 124/2e to that shown on drawing no 124/2f	—	—

To be signed by or for the issuer named above.

Signed A Lane

Amount of Contract Sum	£	1,002,565
± Approximate value of previous instructions	£	320
	£	
± Approximate value of this instruction	£	—
Approximate adjusted total	£	1,002,885

Distribution	☑ Employer	☑ Contractor	☑ Quantity Surveyor	☐ Services Engineer
	☐	☐ Nominated Sub-Contractors	☐ Structural Engineer	☑ File

© 1985 RIBA Publications Ltd

Fig. 13.34 Architect's instruction

Interim certificate

and Direction

Issued by: Lane & Ralph
address: Hogsmill House, Sarah's Drive, Stoneleigh, Surrey

Employer: Henry Electronics Ltd
address: 100 Hart Road London, SW1

Contractor: Porter Construction Ltd
address: 77 Pembroke Road, Kingston, Surrey

Works: Factory and office block
Situated at: Stephen's Industrial Estate, Box Hill, Epsom

Contract dated: 10th October 1989

Serial no: **B** 557657

Interim Certificate no: 1

Job reference: AL/124

Issue date: 14/11/1989

Valuation date: 11/11/1989

Original to Employer

Under the terms of the above mentioned Contract, in the sum of

£ 1,002,565

I/We certify that interim payment as shown is due from the Employer to the Contractor, and

I/We direct the Contractor that the amounts of interim or final payments due to Nominated Sub-Contractors included in this Certificate and listed on the attached *Statement of Retention and of Nominated Sub-Contractors' Values* are to be discharged to those named.

Gross valuation inclusive of the value of Works by Nominated

Sub-Contractors . . . . £ 85,000

Less Retention which may be retained by the Employer as detailed on

the Statement of Retention . . . . £ 3,400

Sub-total £ 81,600

Less total amount stated as due in Interim Certificates previously

issued up to and including Interim Certificate no: £

Amount for payment on this Certificate . . . . £ 81,600

(in words) Eighty-one thousand, six hundred pounds

All amounts are exclusive of VAT

To be signed by or for the issuer named above.

Signed A Lane for Lane & Ralph

Contractor's provisional assessment of total amounts included in above certificate on which VAT will be chargeable £ _____ @ 15 %

This is not a Tax Invoice

© 1985 RIBA Publications Ltd

Fig. 13.35 Interim certificate

Issued by: **Lane & Ralph**
address: **Hogsmill House, Sarah's Drive,
Stoneleigh, Surrey**

Employer: **Henry Electronics Ltd**
address: **100 Hart Road
London SW1**

Contractor: **Porter Construction Ltd**
address: **77 Pembroke Road
Kingston, Surrey**

Works: **Factory and office block**
Situated at: **Stephen's Industrial Estate
Box Hill, Epsom**

Contract dated: **10th October 1989**

Certificate of

**Practical
Completion**

of the Works

Serial no: **MW/12**

Job reference: **AL/124**

Issue date: **20/9/90**

Under the terms of the above mentioned Contract,

I/We certify that Practical Completion of the Works was achieved on:

18th September _____ 19 **90**

To be signed by or for
the issuer named
above.

Signed **A Lane for Lane & Ralph**

The Defects Liability Period will therefore end on:

18th September _____ 19 **90**

Distribution	Original to:	Duplicate to:	Copies to:	
	☑ Employer	☑ Contractor	☑ Quantity Surveyor	☐ Services Engineer
		☐ Nominated Sub-Contractors	☐ Structural Engineer	☑ File

© 1985 RIBA Publications Ltd

Fig. 13.36 Certificate of practical completion

Certificate of
completion of

**Making good
defects**

Issued by: Lane & Ralph
address: Hogomill House, Sarah's Drive
Stoneleigh, Surrey

Employer: Henry Electronics Ltd
address: 100 4 Hart Road
London, SW1

Contractor: Porter Construction Ltd
address: 77 Pembroke Road,
Kingston, Surrey

Works: Factory and office block
Situated at: Stephen's Industrial Estate
Box Hill, Epsom

Contract dated: 10th October 1989

Serial no: MW/13

Job reference: AL/124

Issue date: 10/11/90

Under the terms of the above mentioned Contract,

I/We hereby certify that the defects, shrinkages and other faults specified
in the schedule of defects delivered to the Contractor as an instruction have
in my/our opinion been made good.

This Certificate refers to:

*Delete as
appropriate

*1. The Works described in the Certificate of Practical Completion
Serial no. MW/12 dated 20th September 1990

*2. The Works described in the Certificate of Partial Possession of a relevant
part of the Works
Serial no._____dated_____

To be signed by or for
the issuer named
above.

Signed A Lane for Lane & Ralph

Distribution	Original to:	Duplicate to:	Copies to:	
	☑ Employer	☑ Contractor	☑ Quantity Surveyor	☐ Services Engineer
		☐ Nominated Sub-Contractors	☐ Structural Engineer	☑ File

© 1985 RIBA Publications Ltd

Fig. 13.37 Certificate of making good defects

Issued by: **Lane & Ralph**
address: Hogsmill House, Sarah's Drive, Stoneleigh, Surrey

Employer: Henry Electronics Ltd
address: 100 Hart Road, London SW1

Contractor: Porter Construction Ltd
address: 77 Pembroke Road, Kingston, Surrey

Works: Factory and office block,
Situated at: Stephen's Industrial Estate, Box Hill, Epsom

Contract dated: 10th October 1989

Final Certificate

Serial no: MW / 14

Job reference: AL / 124

Issue date: 13 / 11 / 1990

Original to Employer

Under the terms of the above mentioned Contract,

the Contract Sum adjusted as necessary is . . . . £ 1,025,605

The total amount previously certified for payment to the contractor is . . £ 975,050

The difference between the above stated amounts is . . . . £ 50,555

(in words) Fifty thousand five hundred and fifty five pounds

*Delete as appropriate

and is hereby certified as a balance due* to the Contractor from the Employer/*to the Employer from the Contractor.

All amounts are exclusive of VAT

To be signed by or for the issuer named above.

Signed A Lane for Lane & Ralph

*Delete as appropriate

1 The terms of the Contract provide that the amount shall as from the *14th/21st day after the date of this Certificate be a debt payable from the one to the other subject to any amounts properly deductible by the Employer.

This is not a Tax Invoice

Note: 1 Payment becomes due 14 days after issue where the contract is JCT 80 or MW 80 and 21 days after issue for IFC 84.

© 1985 RIBA Publications Ltd

Fig. 13.38 Final certificate

Words, phrases and abbreviations

14.1 Introduction

This chapter provides a summary, in alphabetical order, of the meaning of the various words, phrases and abbreviations used in the subject of architectural design procedures.

14.2 Words and phrases

Abstracting
The third stage in the preparation of bills of quantities in which similar types of dimensions (i.e. cubical, squared and lineal) are brought together on sheets called the 'abstract'.

Agent
Someone who represents a person or firm in business matters. In a building project the architect acts as the client's agent, and has the authority to spend money on his behalf.

Agre'ment certificate
Certificates granted by an independent testing organisation, called the British Board of Agre'ment, stating that the manufacturer's products have satisfactorily passed agreed tests. Subsequent to the granting of the certificate strict quality control has to be continued.

Arbitration
A technical court to settle disputes which cannot be resolved by the parties involved. The arbitrator is an independent, third person, (often an architect or surveyor) who hears all the arguments, and gives a ruling, which must be accepted by both parties to the dispute.

Architect's certificate
A notice from the architect, generally written on a standard form, informing the employer that he is under a contractual obligation to pay the contractor for work done. See the following for different types of certificates.

Architect's instruction
Further drawings, details and instructions issued by the architect to the contractor, after the issue of the contract documents. They are generally given on a standard form.

Assembly drawing
A drawing which shows how the parts of a building are constructed, and how they meet at junctions. An example of an assembly drawing is a 1:5 detail at the cill position of a window.

Bankruptcy
The state of affairs when a person is unable to meet his debts as they become due. For a limited company, the process of becoming bankrupt is called liquidation.

Billing
The final stage in the preparation of bills of quantities, which consists of writing the bills from previously prepared information (i.e. 'casting' stage) into its final form.

Bills of quantities
A contract document generally prepared by a quantity surveyor to enable the contractor to estimate the cost of a building. It describes and details the materials and labour needed to construct the building shown on the architect's drawings.

British Standards Specification
These are issued by the British Standards Institution to lay down minimum standards for materials and components (e.g. walling blocks and doors) used in the construction and other industries.

Building owner
The traditional term to describe the client in a building project. This term is interchangable with the general term 'client', and the contractual term of 'employer'.

Building regulations
Regulations concerned with safeguarding the safety and health of occupants of completed buildings. They deal with matters such as safe methods of design, standards of construction, and selection and use of materials.

Building surveyor
A specialist in building construction who investigates and reports on buildings, and is often involved in the design, specification and supervisory work for the repair, rehabilitation, alteration and extension of existing buildings.

Building team
Those people who are collectively involved in the design and construction of a building. They consist of the client, architect, quantity surveyor, consulting structural engineer, consulting building services engineer, contractor, including the site manager and foreman, sub-contractors and suppliers, clerk of works and resident engineer.

Bye-laws
Laws made by local authorities and public bodies, under powers given to them by parliament.

Casting
The fourth stage in the preparation of bills of quantities, which consists of adding up similar items previously brought together in the 'abstract' stage.

Civil engineering
The design and construction of structures such as roads, bridges, tunnels, harbours, dams, airstrips, irrigation systems, and similar unroofed structures.

Client
The person for whom a service or product is provided. In the case of a building project, the service is provided by the architect and other members of the design team, and the product is the building provided by the contractor. The term is interchangable with 'employer', which is the term used in the building contract, and the term 'building owner', which is traditional term used to describe the client.

Codes of practice
Code of good practice, issued by the British Standards Institution, to cover workmanship in specific areas – e.g. building drainage, and brick and block masonry.

Collateral warranty
A guarantee which, in the case of a building, commits the architect to guarantee to future purchasers of the building, as well as the original owner, that the building will be fit for the purpose for which it was built.

Common law
Originally meant the law which is common throughout England, as opposed to local

rules. It is now taken to mean the unwritten law – i.e. all law other than the enacted law (or law imposed by legislation).

Component drawing

A drawing which shows the shape, dimensions, assembly and other details of components, such as a window.

Conservation area

An area with particularly attractive or historic features, which is protected under the Town and Country Planning acts against unsuitable development. The local district or county council declares an area to be a conservation area. The aim is to enhance such areas, and planning applications are scrutinised with special care.

Consultant

A person who provides specialist advice and information. In the case of building projects, the term is most likely to refer to structural engineers and building services engineers, who take responsibility for these areas of a project. The term is also used to denote experienced architects (often retired partners) who give advice on architectural and construction matters to architectural practices.

Contingency sum

A sum of money included in the contract price of a building project to cover the cost of extra work which it is not possible to anticipate at the design stage of the project.

Contract

A business agreement between two parties. In the subject under consideration it is between the employer (client) and the contractor (builder).

Corporation tax

A tax imposed by the government, and paid by companies, on their net profits. The actual rate depends on how much profit is made.

Cost control

The process of taking all possible steps to ensure that the final cost of the building is in accordance with the client's requirements and ability to pay. The duty of exercising cost control rests with the design team, particularly the quantity surveyor, and is pursued from the first approximate estimate, throughout the project, until the final account.

Cost limits

The total amount of money the client is prepared to spend on the building he requires.

Cost plan
A plan for allocating the available money among the various elements (e.g. sub-structure, walls, roof, etc.) of the proposed building.

Dayworks
Work which is difficult to measure, price and be included in the bills of quantities in the normal way. The work is listed on daywork sheets, and shows hours worked by various trades, materials and plant used, and any other charges. In practice it means that the contractor recoups all his costs, including a percentage for overheads.

Defects: Liability period
A period, stated in the contract, but usually six months, after the employer takes over the building, when all defects due to faulty materials and workmanship must be made good.

Delays
Circumstances which prevent the contractor from completing the work in accordance with the agreed programme. The delays may be caused by the contractor, employer, architect, or for reasons beyond the control of the parties to the contract.

Design brief
Statement by the client, of the requirements for the building he has commissioned. It will generally include information on the accommodation, quality of construction and finishes, total cost of the project, and the time scale within which he wants the building to be constructed.

Design team
Those members of the building team who are particularly involved in the design, as opposed to the construction aspects of a building project. They are usually considered to be the client, architect, quantity surveyor, consulting structural engineer, and consulting building services engineer.

Development plan
Plan prepared by the local district or county council to protect the environment, and achieve a balanced allocation of the available land to meet the various needs. Among other things it stipulates the type of development (e.g. houses, factories, offices) permitted in a particular area.

Easement
Rights acquired to benefit from someone else's land, such as the right of way over a piece of land; the right to lay and maintain drains under a person's land, and the right of support to a building.

Employer
A legal term used to describe the client, particularly in relation to the building contract. The two terms – 'client' and 'employer' – are interchangable.

Employer's liability insurance
An insurance taken out by the contractor to idemnify the employer for any claims resulting from injury or death of any person on the construction site.

Environment
The strict meaning is 'surrounding objects', but in relation to architectural design procedures it can be taken to mean the things which surround a building or building site, including the climate.

Estimate
A prediction as to the cost of undertaking specified building work. Initially contractors think of this as a net cost, to which overheads and profits etc., are added at the tender stage.

Extension of time
The procedure to extend the date for completion of a building project from that stated in the contract. It also sets back the date on which the contractor is liable to pay damages because he has not completed the building work by the contractual date.

Feedback
The process of learning from experience gained during the course of a building project. Successful and unsuccessful aspects of the project are recorded, and lessons learned for application to future projects.

Final account
The account which is prepared and paid after all building work is completed. It takes into consideration all variations, remeasurement, fluctuations in labour rates and materials prices, and all other factors affecting the total cost of the project. It tells the client what the total cost of the building project is, and how much money remains to be paid to the contractor.

Final certificate
The certificate issued after the final account has been prepared, which releases all outstanding monies due to the contractor after completion of all work, including making good defects. With the introduction of the 1985 Building Regulations the term 'final certificate' is also used to describe the certificate issued by an approved inspector to signify the completion of building work.

Firm
A term which has no legal significance, but is used to denote partners and others carrying on a business together.

Fluctuations clause
A clause in a building contract which allows for a price adjustment to take account of changes in materials and labour costs since the contract was signed.

Freezing of the design
The term used to indicate the stage when the members of the design team jointly agree that there will be no further changes in the design of a proposed building, particularly in respect of its siting, size, shape, and general arrangement.

Handing over
The stage in a building project when the employer takes over the responsibility of the building from the contractor. Although the contractor may still have some items to work to complete at the handing over stage, the employer is legally responsible for the building.

Indemnity insurance
An insurance policy taken out by a professional person, such as an architect, to protect him against claims by his clients for negligence, errors, omissions etc.

Industrial tribunal
Statutory bodies, similar to courts, which pronounce judgements on cases connected with employment law, such as disputes between employers and employees.

Interim certificate
Certificates issued at regular intervals, generally every month, to pay the contractor for work carried out to date, including all materials on site ready for immediate use.

Joint Contracts Tribunal
A body composed of representatives of various bodies concerned with building contracts (e.g. the RIBA, RICS and BEC) who prepare standard forms of building contracts.

Lead-in time
Period of time between the award of a contract to a contractor and the time he actually starts work on site. During the lead-in time the contractor organises his labour, materials and plant, and generally gets ready to begin construction.

Local Authority

An elected body of members forming the council, together with a separate body of paid staff (e.g. planning officers and building control officers) who administer services in a specified area of the UK. They have a separate legal entity from central government, but no powers except those granted to them by the government, such as powers to administer town planning and building regulations.

Location drawing

A drawing which locates and identifies spaces and parts of a building, such as rooms, doors, and drainage. Examples of location drawings are 1:100 plans, elevations and sections.

Main contractor

One of the two parties to a building contract. He has overall responsibility to construct the building, including control of sub-contractors and suppliers.

Making good defects certificate

Certificate issued by the architect authorising a payment to the contractor when all defective work has been made good.

Memorandum of Agreement

A document signed between the client and architect agreeing the conditions of the architect's appointment, including the extent of the services the architect will provide and the fees he will receive.

Microfiche

A small sheet of film bearing a microphotograph – i.e. a photograph reduced to a very small size – of a document.

Multi-discipline practice

A professional firm in which its members are trained and experienced in different skills. In the building industry this could mean for example a firm containing architects, quantity surveyors, structural engineers, building services engineers and town planners.

National building specification

A form of building specification published by the RIBA which uses the CI/SfB coding system, and provides details of materials and workmanship under separate headings.

Negligence

Failure by someone (e.g. in the case of a building contract, the architect) to take the care that should have been taken, and as a result of this carelessness causing damage to another party (e.g. the client).

Nominated sub-contractor
A sub-contractor selected by the architect to carry out specialist work on the site.

Non-nominated contractor
A sub-contractor selected by the contractor (as opposed to the architect) to carry out specialist work on the site. Also given the name of domestic sub-contractor.

Organisational framework
In relation to the design team this term means the breaking down of the team into groups giving each group specific tasks to undertake in order to achieve the overall objectives of the design team.

Practical completion
The stage when the building is completed and in a fit state to be taken over by the employer for its intended use. The defects liability period commences from this date.

Practical completion certificate
The certificate issued by the architect, authorising a payment to the contractor at the practical completion stage.

Pre-contract
The stage of a building project prior to the contractor taking possession of the site and beginning work.

Prime cost
A sum added by the contractor to his tender, to cover work by a nominated sub-contractor, or goods supplied by a nominated supplier.

Production information
The total information, including drawings, schedules and specifications, produced by the design team, to facilitate the erection of the building.

Provisional sum
A sum of money included in the bills of quantities to cover an item for which detailed information is not available at the time the bills are prepared.

Public limited company

A company listed on the Stock Exchange, and able to raise money as required from the general public by selling shares in the company, and to transfer the shares from one investor to another. To be listed, the company must have a stipulated minimum amount of capital.

Quality control

The process of ensuring that the standards set in the drawings, specifications and other contractual documents, for workmanship and materials, are complied with.

Quotation

A firm price given for goods to be supplied, or work which has to be done. Unless the quotation clearly states that the price may be varied, it becomes fixed as soon as it is accepted by the customer. This is different to an estimate, which is considered to represent a probable cost of supplying goods, or undertaking work.

Restrictive covenant

Undertakings to restrict the use of one piece of land so that occupiers of other pieces of land may benefit. An example is not to change the appearance of a building.

Retention

A sum of money deducted from each valuation (see valuation) so as to protect the employer in case things go wrong. The amount is not generally more than 5% of the valuation.

RIBA plan of work

A scheme prepared by the RIBA, showing the content and order of the architect's work. The work is divided into stages, and all significant events are listed. It is fully described in the Architect's Job Book, published by the RIBA.

Samples

A specimen of a product or component, such as a brick, tile or window, which is submitted to and approved by the architect, as being suitable for use in the proposed building.

Sample panel

A specimen of a piece of work, such as a panel of brickwork, which is prepared so that the architect can examine and approve it as being of a suitable standard for use in the proposed building.

Schedules
The presentation of information in a tabulated form for items such as doors, windows, ironmongery, finishes and manholes.

Specification
A document giving a written description of materials to be used, and construction methods to be employed in the erection of a building.

Squaring
The second stage in the preparation of bills of quantities, in which sets of dimensions 'taken off' in the previous stage are multiplied together to obtain squared or cubical values, or left in a lineal form.

Standard Method of Measurement
A document which details the way each item in the bills of quantities should be measured.

Statutory
Something which is required to be done because of written law, such as the building regulations.

Sub-contractor
A person or firm employed to carry out a part of the building work – for example, suspended ceilings or the electrical installation.

Supplier
A person or firm employed to supply goods – for example, for windows or bricks.

Taking off
The first stage in the preparation of bills of quantities in which dimensions taken from drawings are entered onto sheets of paper.

Tender
An offer by a contractor to erect for a specified sum, in a specified time, and under stated conditions, the building work described in the contract bills of quantities, specification and drawings.

Tender documents
Documents supplied to the contractor to enable him to prepare a tender.

Tender figure
The sum of money forming part of the tender.

Tort
A word of French origin meaning 'a wrong'. A tort is a civil wrong imposed by the law, as opposed to contractual liability which is imposed by consent between the parties to a contract. Torts include trespass, nuisance, and negligence.

User requirements
A summary of precisely what type of building and facilities are needed by the proposed occupier of a building.

Valuation
A calculation by the quantity surveyor of the amount due to be paid to the contractor for work done and materials supplied to the site. As interim certificates are generally issued at monthly intervals, valuations will also generally be made every month.

Value added tax
A tax charged by the government on each business transaction involved in supplying goods and services. It is currently charged at 15%.

Variation Order
An addition, omission, or alteration to the contract, issued to the contractor by the architect, generally on a standard form.

14.3 Abbreviations

AI	Architect's Instruction
ARCUK	Architect's Registration Council of the United Kingdom
BBA	British Board of Agre'ment
BEC	Building Employers Confederation
BIAT	British Institute of Architectural Technicians
BQ	Bills of Quantities
BRE	Building Research Establishment
BSI	British Standards Institution
BSS	British Standards Specification
BTEC	Business and Technical Education Council
CAD	Computer Aided Design (or Draughting)
CIBS	Chartered Institution of Building Services
CIOB	Chartered Institute of Building
CI/SfB	Construction Industry/Samarbetskommitten fur Byggnadsfragor (which is Swedish for the Coordinating Committee for the Building Industry).

COW	Clerk of Works
CP	Code of Practice
EEC	European Economic Community
HMSO	Her Majesty's Stationery Office
ICE	Institution of Civil Engineers
ISE	Institution of Structural Engineers
JCT	Joint Contracts Tribunal
LA	Local Authority
NBS	National Building Specification
NFBTE	National Federation of Building Trades Employers
NHBC	National House Builder's Council
NJCC	National Joint Consultative Committee
PAYE	Pay As You Earn
PC	Prime Cost
plc	Public Limited Company
QS	Quantity Surveyor
RE	Resident Engineer
RIBA	Royal Institute of British Architects
RICS	Royal Institution of Chartered Surveyors
SAAT	Society of Architectural and Associated Technicians
SMM	Standard Method of Measurement
VAT	Value Added Tax
VDU	Visual Display Unit
VO	Variation Order

15

Questions

15.1 Introduction

This chapter consists a series of questions which the student, can attempt so as to check whether the contents of the book have been assimilated. If the reader is unable to answer a specific question re-reading the sections of the book indicated in brackets would be advisable.

15.2 Questions

1 Describe the historical development of the architect from his original role, to his present role as leader of the design team (1.2, 2.2, 3.2).

2 Explain the need for a 'design team framework' today (2.3, 3.9).

3. Describe the role of architectural technicians in architects' offices (2.6).

4 Describe how the client's organisational needs may influence the composition of the design team (3.15, 3.16).

5 Describe the different types of architectural practices (3.2, 3.5, 3.6).

6 Explain why good communications are necessary between the various members of the design team (3.10, 3.11, 3.12).

7 Explain the significance of 'professional negligence' (4.2 to 4.13).

8 Describe the legal responsibility of design team members to each other and to the client (2.7).

9 Explain the need for 'indemnity insurance' (2.10).

10 Describe the constraints imposed on a design by the client (7.2, 7.3).

11 Describe the constraints imposed on a design by the site (7.4).

12 Describe the constraints imposed on a design by the environment (7.5).

13 Describe the constraints imposed on a design by 'cost limits' (7.6).

14 Describe the constraints imposed on a design by legal requirements (7.7).

15 Describe the effect of the Building Regulations on a design (7.8).

16 Describe the effect of building engineering services on a design (7.10).

17 Explain what is meant by the term 'organisational framework' (3.5, 3.6).

18 Describe how the client's brief is established (3.15, 3.16, 7.2, 7.3, 10.2, 10.3).

19 Describe what is discussed at pre-contract meetings, and the purpose of such meetings (10.2 to 10.10).

20 Describe different methods of communicating design outcomes to the client (9.2).

21 Explain why it is necessary, at a certain stage of the project, to 'freeze' the design (10.6).

22 Describe the information required to obtain approximate estimates of a project (9.3).

23 Describe the information required to enable competitive tenders to be obtained (9.5).

24 Describe the procedures to be followed to convert a tender into a contract (10.9, 10.10).

25 Briefly describe the items covered by the Pre- contract Stages A to J of the RIBA Plan of Work (10.1 to 10.9).

26 Describe the architect's responsibilities towards the client during the contract stage (2.7, 12.2, 12.3).

27 Describe the importance of quality control during the course of building work (11.2, 11.3).

28 Describe the importance of accurate record keeping during the course of building work (11.15, 11.17, 12.2).

29 Describe how information and instructions are relayed from the design team staff to the site staff during the building process (8.4 to 8.8, 8.11 to 8.15, 11.4, 11.5).

30 Describe the methods of payment for building work (11.6 to 11.9).

31 Briefly describe the items covered by the Contract Stages K to M of the RIBA Plan of Work (12.1 to 12.4).

32 Describe how the progress of work on a construction site is recorded (11.17 to 11.19).

33 Explain why it is important to record things which happen during construction and how this is achieved (11.20).

34 Describe specific information which the contractor has to supply to the architect during the contract period (11.21).

35 Explain the difference between the total cost of a project and the cost value to the client (7.6).

36 Explain how the cost of a job is affected by the building market (7.6).

Bibliography

Architect's Appointment (Conditions of Engagement), RIBA Publications Ltd., 1989

Beaven, Cox, Dry and Males, *RIBA Architect's Jobbook*, RIBA publications Ltd., 1988

Briggs M. S, *Concise Encyclopaedia of Architecture*, J.S. Dent, 1962

Clamp H, *The Shorter Forms of Building Contract*, Blackwell, 1988

Jones N.F. and Bergman D, *The JCTG Intermediate Form of Building Contract*, Blackwell, 1985

Handbook of Architectural Practice and Management, RIBA Publications Ltd., 1980

Lancaster O, *Pillar to Post*, John Murray, 1948

Parris J, *The Standard Form of Building Contract*, Blackwell, 1990

Ray-Jones A and Clegg D, *CI/SfB Construction Indexing Manual*, RIBA publications Ltd., 1976

RIBA Code of Professional Conduct, RIBA Publications Ltd., 1988

RIBA Plan of Work, RIBA Publications Ltd., 1973

Speight and Stone, *AJ Legal Handbook*, Butterworths, 1985

The Building Regulations, Her Majesty's Stationery Office, 1985

The following Joint Contracts Tribunal Standard Forms of Building Contracts are published by the Joint Contracts Tribunal and obtainable from the Building Employers Confederation:

JCT Standard Form, Local Authorities with Quantities, 1980

JCT Standard Form, Local Authorities without Quantities, 1980

JCT Standard Form, Local Authorities, with Approximate Quantities, 1980

JCT Standard Form, Private with Quantities, 1980

JCT Standard Form, Private without Quantities, 1980

JCT Standard Form, Private with Approximate Quantities, 1980

JCT Intermediate Form of Building Contract, 1984

JCT Standard Form of Management Contract, 1984

JCT Minor Work Form, 1988

Recommended reading

British Standard Specifications published by the British Standards Institution.
British Standard Specifications are available for most materials and components used in the building industry. The full list is too long to include here, but details can be obtained from the British Standards Institution.

British Standard Codes of Practice published by the British Stnadards Institution.
Codes of Practice are available covering design and workmanship for most building activities. Again the full list is too long to include here, but details can be obtained from the British Standards

Building Research Establishment Digests published by the BRE. These digests are published each month. They review and assess the effectivness of building techniques and materials.

Fletcher B (Sir), *A History of Architecture*, The Athlone Press, 1975

Law reports published in the technical press. Most technical journals covering the building industry regularly publish law reports on building matters. I particularly recommend the following:
Building Design published by Morgan Grampian plc, weekly
Building published by The Building, weekly.
Standard Method of Measurement of Building Work 7th edition (SMM7), The Royal Institution of Chartered Surveyors, 1988

Tutt and Adler, *AJ Metric Handbook*, Butterworths, 1979

Wessex Price Books, Wessex Publishing Ltd., 1989

Index